gardening neighbours

gardening neighbours

PHILIP McCANN

BⓍXTREE

First published 2001 by Boxtree,
an imprint of Macmillan Publishers Ltd
25 Eccleston Place London SW1W 9NF
Basingstoke and Oxford

www.macmillan.com

Associated companies throughout the world

ISBN 0 7522 6137 1

By arrangement with the BBC

The BBC logo is a trademark of the British Broadcasting Corporation and is used under licence.

BBC logo © BBC 1996

Text copyright © Philip McCann 2001

All photography by Edward Schneider, except pages: 2 © Fran Harper, The Garden Picture Library; 6, 8, 9, 10, 12 (top), 13, 15, 17, 19, 21, 23, 25, 27 © BBC/Mike Kelly and Richard Kendal; 95 © Alan Gould, The Garden Picture Library.

Garden designs on pages 13-27 © Ali Ward and Chris Beardshaw

Designed by seagulls

Gardening Neighbours is a Lifestyle and Features, BBC Birmingham production.
Executive Producer - Patrick Flavelle
Producer - Karen Mackinder
Series Director - Attracta McLaughlin

9 8 7 6 5 4 3 2

A CIP catalogue record for this book is available from the British Library.

Printed by New Inter Litho Spa, Milan

Before starting any task, you should be confident that you know how to use all the tools and equipment described in the book safely. The publishers and the author cannot accept any legal responsibility or liability for accidents and damage arising from the use of any items mentioned, or in the carrying out of any of the projects described in this book.

contents

fore**word**

it seems that our appetite for all things gardening at present is insatiable. Everywhere you look there are books, magazines, television programmes and experts offering advice. This book, however, is different. The gardens covered here are real people's gardens. It really doesn't matter if you are starting with a clean slate, as we did on *Gardening Neighbours*, or trying to find space in your already overflowing garden for a new feature. Without a doubt, there are horticultural gems within these pages to help and guide you.

The challenges and principles of designing and implementing a garden are the same irrespective of the size of the plot – the important thing is the pleasure you gain from producing a garden that is well designed, easy to live with and a joy to be in. The *Gardening Neighbours* gardens have different design solutions because not only do we as designers approach design from different perspectives but we also aim to design gardens that complement our clients' characters and satisfy their needs. It was also refreshing to have another designer over the wall to throw ideas at – and, in fact, we both enjoyed a summer of good-natured banter. We would even go so far as to say that we admired each other's finished designs.

Don't be fooled by this book's glossy photographs – there are no quick-fix gardening solutions. Creating gardens, especially on such challenging sites, requires a significant effort. As self-confessed garden virgins, our neighbours were amazed at the work required to create great gardens, but when the finished schemes emerged they had a huge sense of achievement and pride in the results.

For our gardening neighbours we hope that this is just the start of a love affair with gardening. We have both gardened since we were children and we know how infectious it can be. No doubt we have infected them with the curse of never being able to pass a garden centre without 'just popping in'.

In *Gardening Neighbours* we hope we have shown that it doesn't matter if you own half of Warwickshire or a few square metres, design style and impact are only limited by your imagination. For both of us success in gardening should not be judged on the rarity of your plants or the proportions of your pergola but on the immense joy both the process and finished article can give you.

If we can offer one piece of gardening advice it is to be an individual in your garden and grow plants that you love in a way that pleases you.

intro**duction**

many people believe that a garden is an extension of the home. For the gardening neighbours, their homes are very much extensions of their gardens.

They had it all to do when they took over their patches of soil from the builders: there was nothing much except rubble, compacted earth and a BBC film crew every weekend for five months. With the help of top garden designers Chris Beardshaw and Ali Ward, the plots were transformed into stunning, innovative and dazzling gardens.

The *Gardening Neighbours* gardens presented Chris and Ali with eight opportunities to stretch their design skills, flair and practical knowledge. All of them have clay soil that becomes water-logged in the rain and bakes hard in the sun. Four of the gardens face south, with glorious sun all day long. The remaining four face north and are shaded during part of the day. The designs and their implementation were not easy, but the results are spectacular. To make Chris and Ali work extra hard, each of them had two north-facing gardens and two south-facing ones to create.

Tackling projects from scratch allowed the neighbours to learn about every aspect of gardening. From drawing up a list of likes and dislikes, creating a lawn, constructing a water feature, planting a container and placing a statue in the correct place, to the triumphant firming of workable soil around a plant in a

The gardening neighbours' north-facing gardens are on the right, gardens 1 to 4 running from top to bottom; the south-facing gardens are on the left, gardens 5 to 8 running from top to bottom.

The gardening neighbours are ready for action.

gorgeous, flower-filled border, the gardening neighbours did the lot.

Even if you already have a garden, or have moved into a house with an established design, there is still plenty to have a go at. The whole plot can be redesigned if you have the time and inclination, or you can just tinker with a corner to make your garden look a little bit brighter. And that's the beauty of gardening. You can do as much or as little as you want.

Whatever you decide to do, the only rule worth remembering is that it's your garden. It should reflect what you want and it should do what you want it to. If this means giving a gnome a home, then good for you. If it means creating an amazing wavy lawn full of fun and style, then power to your mower. This rule was uppermost in both Chris and Ali's minds when they started the projects with the gardening neighbours. There is no point in forcing a labour-intensive garden on a couple who haven't the time to work in it all day, and who only want to relax and enjoy it. Matching a design to the garden owner is a much-sought-after skill.

Layer upon layer of interest is loaded onto the first sketches until the final design is produced. But a garden is never really finished. The fact that plants grow, or will grow if planted and cared for, means a garden is constantly on the move, evolving, revealing more and more every day. There should always be time to sit or stand back and admire your creation. Becoming a slave to it is surely a cardinal sin of gardening.

Once the design is thought through, the practical aspects have to be considered. It's all very well wanting to grow sun-loving plants, but if your garden is plunged into shade for most of the day this may prove unfeasible. It is also worth bearing in mind that gardeners are not alone in their gardens. They are merely curators of a small patch of nature, and should learn to work with the natural elements to create a harmonious plot.

Gardens, gardeners and their neighbours are all individuals. But individuals make up a team and the gardening neighbours formed a close-knit gardening community. They got to know each other through creating their gardens, a bond that will last forever.

The first question you should ask yourself when inheriting a garden, be it new, established or something in between, is: 'What do I want the garden to do for me?'

Once you have answered that, you can make anything happen.

design

design *v*. conceive, create, fabricate, fashion, invent, originate, think up.

a garden is a personal affair, and designing your own plot of paradise is a chance to express your creative thoughts and ideas. The *Gardening Neighbours* gardens started off naked, devoid of any inhibitions. Rectangles of bare earth were all that designers Chris and Ali had to work with. This can be a good thing, with no existing features getting in the way of the master plan, although established trees and hedges can create an important feeling of maturity. But where on earth do you begin designing a garden, whether from new or for an already cultivated plot?

Both Chris and Ali have creative instincts that enable them to transform ideas and thoughts into beautiful gardens, and each of the distinctive *Gardening Neighbours* ones bears testament to their skills. Having a go at designing your own plot can be daunting, but it needn't be. Think of your garden as a room. You had no difficulty choosing the wallpaper, so why should fencing be a problem? You had no quandaries over whether to have carpets or wooden flooring, so deciding between decking or slabs will be a cinch. And the plants in your garden are like your ornaments, collected over years and each one bringing with it a glorious memory.

Imagine you are moving into a new house, a completely empty shell. You would relish the challenge of designing and decorating it, and your garden is nothing different. Follow a few guidelines and you can achieve more than you think.

assess**your**garden

The first stage of garden design is the assessment of your plot. Make a note of all your observations as this will help with the design when you are poring over books late at night. It will also help the designer if you choose to delegate the work to a professional.

Chris's design converges on a central panel and is executed to perfection.

- Determine whether your garden is sunny or shady, or a combination of both. You will need to do this over a period of time as a garden that is in sunshine in the morning may be plunged into shade as the sun moves round. Check to see where the sun rises in the morning and sets at night as this will give you the orientation of your garden and help you to decide the kind of plants you can grow and where to situate certain features. The four south-facing *Gardening Neighbours* gardens have the problem of sun all day long in a sunny summer, whereas the north-facing ones are very much in the shade most of the day.
- Note whether or not your garden is exposed to wind and, if it is, the direction the breezes whistle in from. Ask neighbours about their experiences, and ask them about frost problems. It could save months of waiting for autumn to find out the effect frost has on your garden.
- Check the soil not only for clay and sand content, but also to see whether or not it drains freely. Use the checks described in 'Plants for Every Garden' to categorize it. This is invaluable information when you are selecting the right plants for your garden.
- Make a visual check of how sloped your garden is or, as in the case of the gardening neighbours, how flat. Again, this will help a designer to build in levels to make the plot interesting, and will also give you an indication of whether steps or terracing will be needed – and whether you need to pay particular attention to Chapter 2, 'Construction'.
- Take accurate measurements of the size of the garden, and if you are employing a designer, obtain a precise value of its gradient. This detail will ensure correct construction of any possible steps.
- Make a note of any existing features, good and bad, and any access points to drains or amenities.

This is quite a list, but everything in it will be helpful in producing a garden you'll be proud of. After all, no matter how much fun you have designing and creating it, you don't want to be doing this every year.

Ali's design is personal to the gardening neighbours and looks stunning.

The following pages feature Chris and Ali's early conceptual drawings for
the gardening neighbours, along with photographs of the completed gardens.

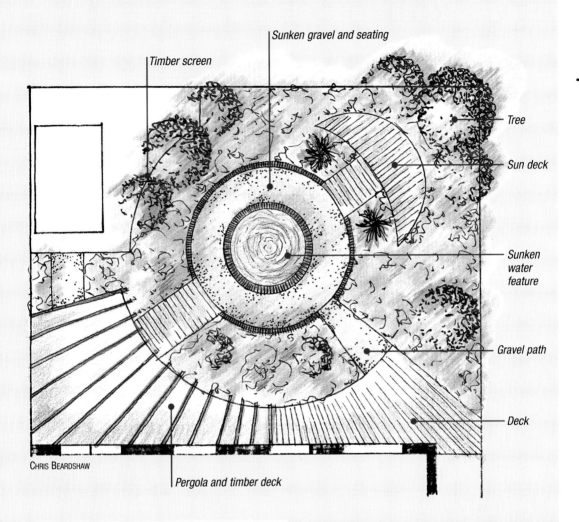

Timber screen

Sunken gravel and seating

Tree

Sun deck

Sunken
water
feature

Gravel path

Deck

CHRIS BEARDSHAW

Pergola and timber deck

do's**&**don'ts
designing**a**water**feature**

✔ **do** design a water feature to be in scale with the rest of
your garden. The Trevi fountain is certainly inspiring, but
best left in Rome for the time being.

✗ **don't** design deep water features if children or animals
use the garden.

✔ **do** position fountains out of wind to avoid water loss.

✗ **don't** put a noisy water feature near a neighbour's fence.
If you have no choice, make sure you can turn it down.

✔ **do** plan the location of a water feature from the
beginning of the design process to avoid excessive
disruption when laying pipes and cables.

make**lists**

Back in from the cold, with your tape measure tucked away, you can now settle down and discuss your thoughts and ideas with other users of the garden, or your designer. Ali Ward got to know the neighbours, understanding their expectations and desires for the gardens. 'I spend time sketching ideas and variations on themes. Sometimes a design comes easily and I know I have got it right as soon as I start to draw. Others are harder to do and I end up with two or three designs to narrow down to just one,' says Ali. Chris Beardshaw has a different approach and finds 'it is possible to very quickly visualize how spaces can be either created or divided down so establishing distinctive character areas with a hierarchy of not only scale but also impact on the senses'.

'For me the most important thing is to look at the site and get a feel for the opportunities offered'
Chris Beardshaw

To allow your ideas to crystallize, write down everything you want. This could include a water feature, decking, a pergola, a swinging hammock, plenty of cottage-garden flowers or a summer house. The gardening neighbours did this, with one stipulating a conservatory. It is vital to get this information on paper as everything can then be planned before the project starts. Imagine the disruption to planting and newly laid stone flooring if you decide on a conservatory once everything else has been completed.

Write down how much time you can spend in the garden, and what you want to be doing in that time. If mowing is your thing make a note of this. One of the neighbours wanted a lawned area he could cherish and manicure, so Chris ensured this was included in his garden. Another wanted theirs to be child-friendly, and this gave Ali the information to create a magnificent garden.

It is also helpful to make a list of everything you definitely don't want in the garden. The gardening neighbours' lists of unwanted items were interesting, with one couple insisting that decking was banned, another stating an abhorrence of pampas grass and a third who wanted to shirk any kind of work.

What the lists do is focus your wants and desires and highlight the aspects of gardening that just aren't for you. They help a designer to get it right from the start – and also help you realize how feasible your garden is going to be. It would be unfair to everyone connected with its design to expect them to include everything on your wanted list. If they did it would probably look like an indigestible mass of vegetation, stone and chippings. Prioritize to help create a workable plan.

Finally, make a list of the items that need to be removed. For the gardening neighbours, this included builders' rubble and bits of discarded central-heating pipes. In an established garden about to undergo an overhaul it could include old sheds, overgrown plants or unwanted crazy paving. Bear in mind that trees add maturity to a garden and may just need a prune rather than uprooting.

design**checklist**
- Survey and assess your garden.
- Make a list of what you want and don't want.
- Decide whether existing features stay or go.
- Decide on positions for pipes, cables and new drainage.
- Ensure the garden has different levels, and draw in steps and terracing if required.
- Design in features that may be eyesores but are essential, such as compost and rubbish bins.
- Position ornamental features on the design.
- Overlay a planting plan.
- Draw up your work-in-progress designs and make copies for any contractors, friends or family involved in the project.
- Start up the excavator and set to work.

do's**&**don'ts
construction**design**

✓ **do** design all construction work before embarking on planting, lawn-laying and flooring projects.

✗ **don't** design features that will be too physically demanding. All aspects of design and gardening should be fun. Avoid over-exertion if you aren't used to manual labour.

✓ **do** design ambitious projects – the specialized tools that can be hired make anything possible.

✗ **don't** design and attempt to build any construction projects that may involve skills that are beyond you.

✓ **do** make sure a construction project is in the right place and that you will continue to be happy with its position. Moving a patio every year is tiring and expensive.

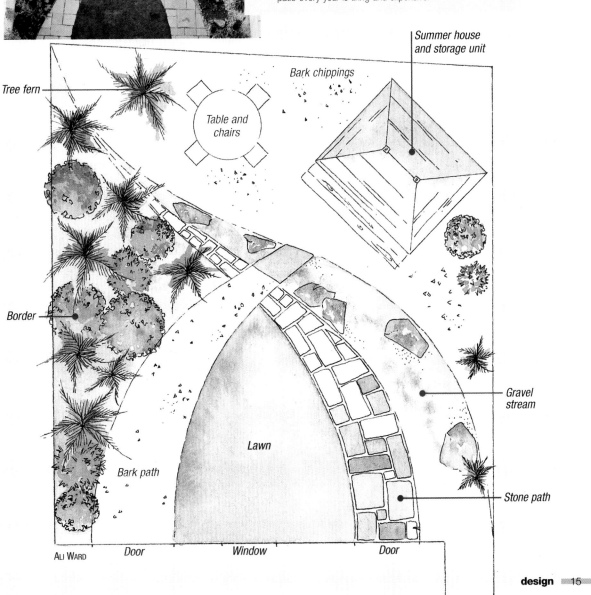

Tree fern

Summer house and storage unit

Bark chippings

Table and chairs

Border

Gravel stream

Lawn

Bark path

Stone path

ALI WARD   Door   Window   Door

design**inspirations**

Inspiration can be gleaned from anywhere and everywhere. All you need to do is keep your eyes open and soak up ideas. Television series are a wonderful source, and books, magazines and other people's gardens are fantastic at providing the seeds of an inspired design. Of course, straightforward copying is fine, but remember that your plot in northern Scotland may not enjoy the conditions that create a gorgeous herbaceous border in the south of England. Rather like fashion shows and clothes, it isn't necessarily the actual details that are the thing to be looking at, but the trends, the colour schemes, the textures. Go back to your own plot and re-create the look according to your local conditions.

> **'The inspiration for all my designs is always the people who own the garden'**
> *Ali Ward*

The large flower shows are showcases for superb designs and are always worth studying for inspiration. One of the *Gardening Neighbours* couples created a scrapbook of their favourite ideas, making Ali's life very much easier when it came to interpreting their likes and dislikes. Garden 4, with its stunning circular decking garden, was the result. Ali Ward gets the inspirations for her superb designs from 'the people who own the gardens. I can never design a garden unless I know all about the people who will use it. Even when I design a show garden I invent owners to design for,' she says.

But inspiration can come from the unlikeliest of places. After idly dropping a pebble into a pond and observing the tiny waves it created, Chris came up with the innovative wavy lawn design in Garden 3. The very pebble he used was the catalyst for a commission to create the beautiful sculpture in Garden 6. Two fantastic ideas from a spare moment near a pond is sheer genius. Chris sees the design challenge as 'blending ingredients. Some of these will come from the clients, some will be extracted from shapes and forms on site, some from the char-

> **'Not all gardens should be constrained by convention otherwise they are destined to become irrelevant to the time'**
> *Chris Beardshaw*

acter inherent in the location or on site and still others will be ideas and concepts which I have been exploring independently usually in some abstract form.'

Gardens can remind you of the past, and one family wanted to reflect their heritage somewhere in their garden. As a result of Ali's creative skill the sensational mosaic in Garden 5 reflects not only the clear blue sky, but Mogul architecture as well.

The unfurling of a tree fern has spawned many design ideas.

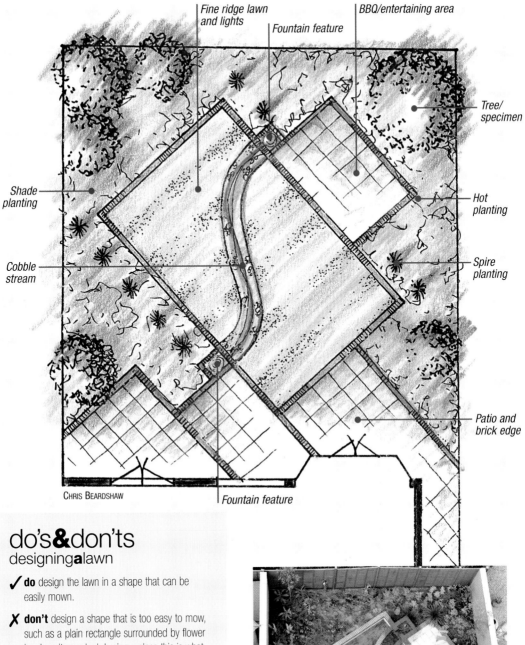

Fine ridge lawn and lights

Fountain feature

BBQ/entertaining area

Tree/ specimen

Shade planting

Hot planting

Cobble stream

Spire planting

Patio and brick edge

CHRIS BEARDSHAW

Fountain feature

do's&don'ts
designing**a**lawn

✓ **do** design the lawn in a shape that can be easily mown.

✗ **don't** design a shape that is too easy to mow, such as a plain rectangle surrounded by flower borders. It may look boring, unless this is what you really want.

✓ **do** make sure the surface is relatively clear of obstacles such as statues and water features. They only make mowing more difficult and time-consuming.

✗ **don't** put an area of lawn in deep shade. Use your design flair to put something else in sunless positions.

✓ **do** design a clear-cut edge around the lawn.

✗ **don't** run the lawn straight up to a wall.

layers**of**interest

The total beauty of a well-designed garden can't be taken in at one sitting. Every time you look at it you should notice another feature, be intrigued as to what is beyond a well-placed trellis, statue, water feature or hedge. So before you start designing, imagine layer upon layer of interest in your bare plot of earth.

The *Gardening Neighbours* gardens started off as flat as pancakes. Different physical levels had to be created. The circular water feature in Garden 1 is below soil level, and the steps created in the child-orientated Garden 7 raise that particular garden. Both these examples required movement of soil, with tons of extra soil required in the children's garden to bring it above the ground level of the house. This can all be done by hand, or heavy digging machinery can be hired. Start thinking about levels before

the**construction**plan

The first plan is often the outline of the garden, drawn to scale with existing features that you want to keep sketched in position. Draw in changes in level, and steps or slopes if easy access is required to any part of the garden. Add access to taps, drains or plugs and you have the start of your drawn design. It is best to include all the construction aspects from the beginning. It is also a great idea to actually do the construction before tackling the planting and laying the lawn.

If you want a conservatory, greenhouse or shed plan them in at this stage. Details such as the placement of compost and rubbish bins need to be considered. If you leave this until the end they may well be squeezed into unsuitable places or, worse still, right in the eyeline, ruining the design. Functional structures and features don't necessarily need to be out of the way, which could make it awkward to get to them and result in underuse and neglect. There are ways of disguising less than beautiful compost bins if they need to be situated near the house, convenient for vegetable waste from the kitchen. The summer house in Garden 2 was certainly not hidden away. It is a main feature of the garden and therefore beautifully styled.

Lighting extends the interest of a garden, and generally requires electricity. At this stage you need to allow for cables and outdoor sockets. Design a number of sockets into your garden as the final lighting scheme often can't be finalized until the plants are in place and the best effects can only be seen through experimentation. After checking the drainage of your soil, decide whether artificial drains are needed. Think long and hard about these as they involve massive upheaval and shouldn't be undertaken lightly.

planting as the caterpillar tracks of an excavator will decimate your delphinium display.

A garden also has to work hard every month of the year. Summer was a popular choice for the gardening neighbours as it's when most leisure time is spent outdoors, but some interest during the rest of the year is important and plants play a vital role in creating this. There is a plant flowering, changing colour or producing berries in every garden, in every month. Evergreen plants are essential if you want to avoid looking at bare fencing in autumn and winter.

Once this backbone has been installed, there is another level of interest – almost subliminal design details, such as the candles hanging from the walls in Garden 5 that create a restful atmosphere around a mosaic surrounded by medicinal plants.

The backbone, a mix of plants and the details all add up to a beautiful garden. Make notes and begin to sketch your ideas. They don't have to be works of art as every stage in the design is merely work in progress. In fact, a garden design is always changing as you decide that a plant is in the wrong place, a hanging basket would add so much beauty to a stark pergola or another row of edging bricks would make the lawn look sensational.

flatgardens

- Create different levels, as Chris and Ali did in most of the *Gardening Neighbours* gardens. This may mean excavating tons of soil or importing more to raise levels.
- Use the space above the garden by planting trees, or building a raised structure like the children's playhouse in Garden 7.

steeply**sloped**gardens

- Terracing or steps make a steep slope manageable and safe.
- Avoid turfing or sowing grass seed on steep slopes as maintenance is difficult.
- Look for ground-cover plants that require little or no maintenance.

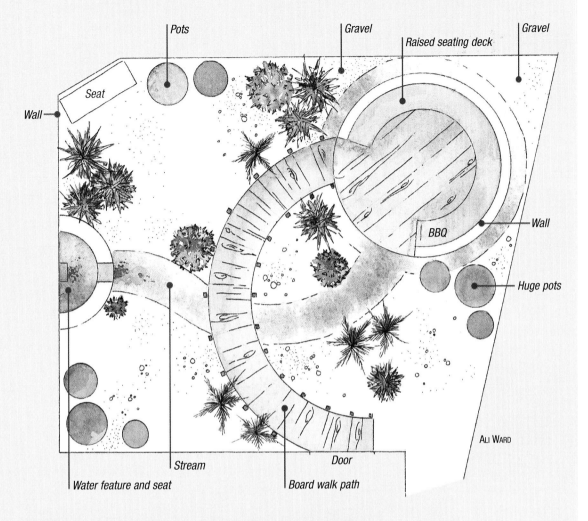

Pots

Gravel

Raised seating deck

Gravel

Seat

Wall

Wall

BBQ

Huge pots

ALI WARD

Stream

Door

Water feature and seat

Board walk path

do's**&**don'ts
designing**with**ornaments

✓ **do** include ornaments in your garden as they add detail and form.

✗ **don't** position ornaments so that they block a view. Move them around the garden to find more favourable positions.

✗ **don't** only use readily available ornaments. Trawl antique shops and other retailers for ones that are suited to your garden.

✓ **do** design lighting into your garden to extend the time you spend in it.

✓ **do** use local materials if possible, as they will blend with your house and surroundings.

gardenfeatures

Features in the *Gardening Neighbours* gardens include a fountain, a summer house, well-placed pots, a boulder or two, a mosaic, a pebble sculpture, a children's playhouse and a statue. Add to that lot benches, pergolas and conservatories, and 'features' becomes an eclectic group with all the individual elements having one thing in common: with Chris and Ali's creative touch, they add to the overall garden picture. It sounds easy to do – anyone can plonk a bench near a chamomile lawn – but a feature in the wrong place can easily destroy a lot of innovative design work.

A room in a house usually has a focal point such as a fireplace. Mimic this elementary design skill by carefully placing, for example, a pebble sculpture to capture the attention and then lead the eye around the garden. Features provide an opportunity for the eye to rest, to settle and then move on. Without such a resting place your eye wouldn't know where to start or, for that matter, where to finish.

You may not need to provide a feature as one may already be present in or around your garden. The *Gardening Neighbours* gardens are bound on the sides by fencing and walls, so features are needed within the plots. There are no planning regulations to stop you using a distant tree or even a complete view – some gardens open onto landscapes where mature trees may grow in magnificent splendour – to make your garden appear bigger and part of the surrounding countryside. Views are vital and may be as simple as a tree or an awe-inspiring contour of a hill. Use them if possible, and run a path in their direction from the starting point in your garden to your boundary. The most important view is from your house onto your own garden, so plan the main thrust of your design around a well-used window. However, never present the entire garden at a glance. Use features and planting to create rooms within it, so that the eye is always intrigued as to what is going to happen next.

long**narrow**gardens

- Make a long narrow garden appear wider by placing mirrors along its sides to reflect it back on itself. This will also increase the light levels in a shady garden.
- Position the patio at a 45° angle to the long axis of the garden. Your eye will naturally focus on the mid-point of the axis, as opposed to taking the easy, lazy and direct route to the end wall in the distance.
- Divide the plot into smaller garden rooms with features, trellis or fencing. Hedging is great for providing a living dividing line.

wide**shallow**gardens

- Sculptures, pots and ornaments come into their own in a wide shallow garden. Well positioned, away from the boundary at the end of the shortest axis, they allow the eye to rest and scan the garden.
- Mirrors placed at the end of the plot will reflect the short length back, making the garden appear longer.
- Use a trompe l'oeil painting to trick the eye into thinking there is a stunning vista or garden beyond a wall. It can be painted directly onto a wall, or on wooden board that can be hung on brickwork or fencing.

getting**around**

Like a good book, your garden needs a start, a beginning and, hopefully, a happy ending. Or take inspiration from any successful supermarket. You walk in and have to look at everything in the shop before being allowed out. Design your garden in a similar vein and you won't go too far wrong.

Each *Gardening Neighbours* garden is entered by a narrow alley along the side of the house. All the alleys are dark, but the garden stages are clearly lit by sunlight, drawing the visitor into a theatre of plants and features. At night artificial lighting takes over and the gardens are irresistible.

Every garden has a definite route, with child-friendly Garden 7 almost signposted through archways. Ali created a relatively simple garden yet packed it with quality design principles. Garden 1, with its impressive centrally located water feature, allows the visitor, and eye, a clear route to the water and around the seating area onto the half-moon decking area for a barbecue and a refreshing drink. The complete garden is therefore viewed on the journey through Chris's stunning design.

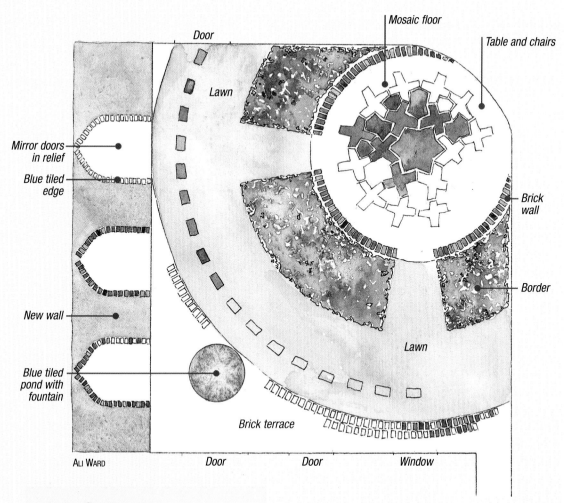

Mosaic floor

Table and chairs

Door

Lawn

Mirror doors in relief

Blue tiled edge

Brick wall

New wall

Border

Blue tiled pond with fountain

Lawn

Brick terrace

ALI WARD

Door

Door

Window

do's&don'ts
designing**for**problem**areas**

✓ **do** include all the necessary problem features, such as a washing line, compost bin and rubbish bin when you start to design your garden.

✗ **don't** design features that will cause problems later on. A large summer house will cast shade and drip water onto surrounding grass. If a summer house is in, grass is out.

✓ **do** make sure you know where drain covers are positioned before designing flooring.

✗ **don't** hope that fencing will hide all the problem areas. Think about positioning plants in front of them, or nearby, to take the eye away.

✓ **do** design with a full knowledge of who or what is using the garden. This eliminates surprise problems later on in the life of the garden.

colour

If there is one aspect of garden design that is guaranteed to spark debate, discussion and disagreement, it's colour. There are gardens, much visited and revered, that are comprised of plants with white flowers, and only white ones. Others are based on blue, with blue plants growing against blue walls under a Portuguese-blue sky. Yet others mix and match colours like an explosion at a paint factory. Each of the owners is delighted with their particular garden, and that is what really counts.

There are rules within garden design that govern which colour goes with what, but, as with all rules, they are made for breaking. However, it is an indisputable fact that certain colours do help to create moods. Ali designed Garden 5 to contain predominantly yellow flowers and foliage. The objective, after consultation with the couple concerned, was to create relaxing surroundings full of medicinal plants. The seating area crowns what is a gorgeous garden that has year-round interest and masses of yellow. The conclusion from this is that yellow is mellow and certainly relaxing. 'A yellow planting scheme was a necessary design element to counterbalance the bold blue wall and cobalt blue

mosaic tiles. When you use strong colours and features in the hard landscaping of a project, you must use the same courage in your planting choices,' explains Ali Ward. If you want to convey a hot, fiery, exciting, vivacious mood choose lots of reds and oranges.

> **'Colour themes work well in most gardens, but it is best to use a range of shades within your chosen colour'**
> *Ali Ward*

Blue is used extensively in the *Gardening Neighbours* gardens as it allows the colours of plants to express themselves. It may be coincidence, but nature's popular colour is that of the sky, which is occasionally, very occasionally, blue. 'It is possible to use the full range of hues in the garden as you would indoors as the principles are

the same. A cool blue happens to aid the creation of a calm relaxing atmosphere; it also associates well with lush green foliage,' says Chris Beardshaw. Starkly contrasting colours work well together, with blue and yellow clashing in an agreeable way on the walls and fencing of Garden 1.

Interior designers use swatches to check the effect of combining particular colours. Do the same when you design your garden by using cut flowers. Do the yellow daffodils really go with the blue *Muscari*, both available in spring from florists? Do the red dahlias and vibrant red-hot pokers really work as you want them to? In a small space lots of different colours may create a claustrophobic feel. It's safer to combine wide ranges of colour in larger borders or gardens.

But your garden is yours so experiment with colour, ignore the rules and regulations, and stamp your personality on your design. If a combination of pink, orange, red and white work for you, then go for it.

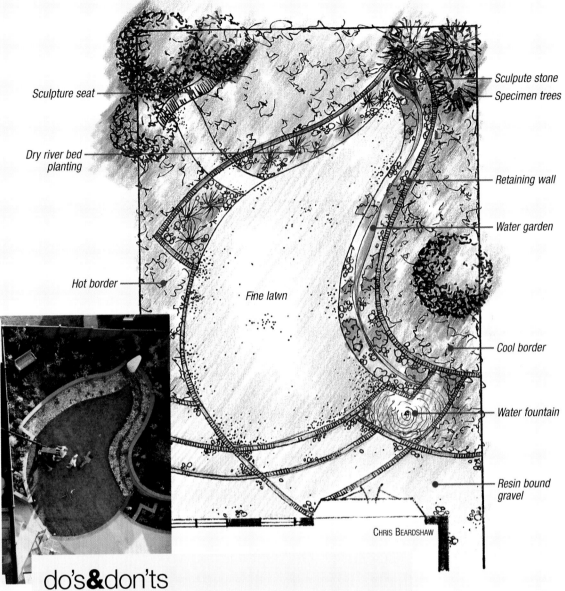

Sculpture seat

Sculpute stone

Specimen trees

Dry river bed planting

Retaining wall

Water garden

Hot border

Fine lawn

Cool border

Water fountain

Resin bound gravel

CHRIS BEARDSHAW

do's**&**don'ts
designing**with**plants

✓ **do** design in the knowledge that plants grow – after all, that is why you spend so much time worrying about them on frosty nights.

✓ **do** space plants out to avoid forcing them into competition for water, light and nutrients.

✗ **don't** use massive specimen plants just because they instantly cover a large area. Smaller plants usually get off to a quicker start once they're out of their pots.

✓ **do** include your favourite plants in a planting scheme. A garden should always be a personal affair.

✗ **don't** design a plan that has every plant you like crammed into the plot. This will detract from your real favourites. Be strong and prioritize, if you can.

✓ **do** make sure trees are away from any houses – yours and your neighbours'. The planting distance from a house should be the same as the eventual height of the tree to avoid problems with roots.

texture**and**scent

Touch is often the forgotten sense in garden design, but is easily incorporated by including touchy-feely plants and features. The smooth pebble sculpture in Garden 6 will eventually become worn by the multitude of caresses bestowed upon it by both owners and visitors. It's impossible to resist the temptation to run delicate fingers through the airy foliage of bamboo growing seductively in Garden 3. Place textured plants near a pathway or route through your garden and stroke them as you pass by.

Scent, smell, perfume or whiff – whichever is your preference – is essential in a total garden design. Sitting beneath an arbour or pergola clothed in honeysuckle, the air misted with intoxicating perfume, is something every gardener should experience for at least two months of every year. Roses are unsurpassable scent-makers and even some conifers, *Thuja* species in particular, have a delightful fruity aroma redolent of scrumping for apples. Place lavender near a pathway and get an immediate relaxing blast of aromatherapy when you return home after a tense day at the office or factory. Ali created the ultimate sniffy border in Garden 7, designed with children in mind. The mint, lavender, thyme and sage are all safe to touch and great to smell.

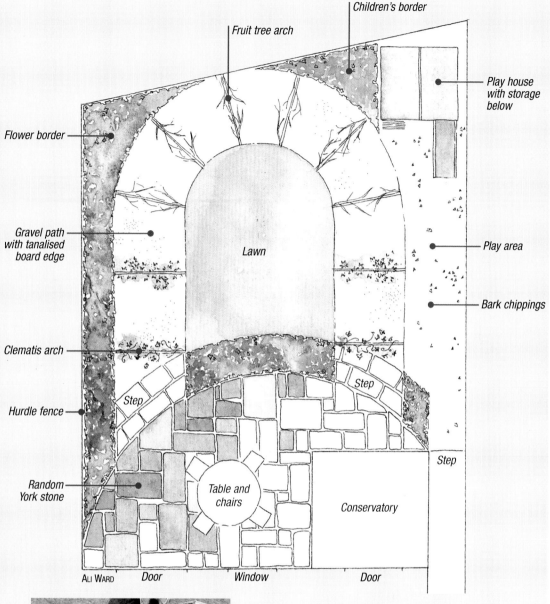

Children's border

Fruit tree arch

Play house with storage below

Flower border

Play area

Gravel path with tanalised board edge

Lawn

Bark chippings

Clematis arch

Step

Step

Hurdle fence

Step

Random York stone

Table and chairs

Conservatory

ALI WARD   Door

Window

Door

do's**&**don'ts
designing**a**children's**garden**

✓ **do** design safety into every part of a children's garden.

✗ **don't** design a garden that children have to behave in. Give them room to explore and investigate.

✓ **do** include safe hideaways and a place they can call their own.

✗ **don't** give children a miserable piece of soil in the darkest corner of the plot for their garden; failure will be guaranteed.

✓ **do** design a fun garden.

makeaplantingplan

People shy away from creating their own planting plans through fear of getting them wrong. However, by reading up on a few plants, such as the crackers described in Chapter 4 'Plants', and following a few guidelines anyone can create a masterful plan. Mark your planting plan on tracing paper and place over your basic structured plan.

Think of your garden in different layers. Study each layer, from the top canopy of leaves down to ground-cover plants or mulches at soil level. This will automatically create a structure. Focus the eye on a striking feature within a planting scheme. This may be a plant in an outstanding colour or with leaves of a different texture or shape, or a container stuffed with brazen bedding plants. In any one border, plant some shrubs that will retain their leaves throughout winter to ensure an evergreen backbone.

Position plants of outstanding architectural beauty, such as the bamboo in Garden 3, close to a plain painted wall. The shadows they cast on a sunny day are magical. This is also a great way to decorate a boring wall without resorting to trellis or fencing. Even the shadow of a leaf falling on a rock can add an infinite amount of beauty to a garden.

Plants clothe a design and can accentuate or detract from the main theme. Straight, formal lines with strong geometry will be ruined by soft, billowing plants, which will cloud the edges and make the whole scene informal. Likewise, a cottage-garden style with blowsy flowers, blurs of foliage and a cotton-wool feel doesn't lend itself to straight rows of clipped box hedging.

Use odd numbers of plants – one if you're on a limited budget, but three or five are a great way to quickly make a clump look established. Don't cram them together; remember, they will grow into each other and create a large specimen in no time at all. Always note the planting distances on the labels, and if plants have a spread of 60cm (2ft), plant them 60cm (2ft) apart.

Add hidden surprises to your garden with both spring- and summer-flowering bulbs. Unless you want them to be absolutely in keeping with a formal design, plant them in irregular clumps or patches. They will look more natural, as if they have been in your garden for years, and will add colour when you have probably forgotten about them. Bulbs such as daffodils and tulips that flower in spring are planted in autumn. Summer-flowering bulbs, tubers and corms such as dahlias and gladioli are planted in spring.

As your garden evolves over a number of years certain plants will become dominant and take over. Others will grow large and cast shade, and will need to be cut back or completely removed. Don't be dismayed. Rather than being a negative aspect, changes like these are a testament to your skill as a designer and plantsperson. They also give you an opportunity to inject fresh zest into a border.

frompapertoplot

Once you are happy with your designs, your drawings and your planting schemes, it's time to translate the whole lot into a garden.

Before setting about your soil with an excavator, mark any features that are not already in your garden on the plot itself. Take a close look at their positions from different angles. The way sunlight or artificial lighting plays on a statue will create shadows on the ground and shaded areas on the statue itself. A quick tweak here or there could make all the difference to the design. Mark out contour lines with sand, by bending and shaping hosepipes or by using specially formulated, non-toxic spray paint.

Before planting trees and shrubs, place them on the soil and take a step back to see how they look from close by. Then view them from all over the garden. Go to an upstairs window and look down on your proposed planting plan. Once you're happy with it, get cracking with the spade. Never rush this stage of design as all the hard work put into soil improvement, positioning features and siting electrical sockets will come to nothing if the plants are in the wrong place.

Only when everyone is happy with the design can you start up the excavator.

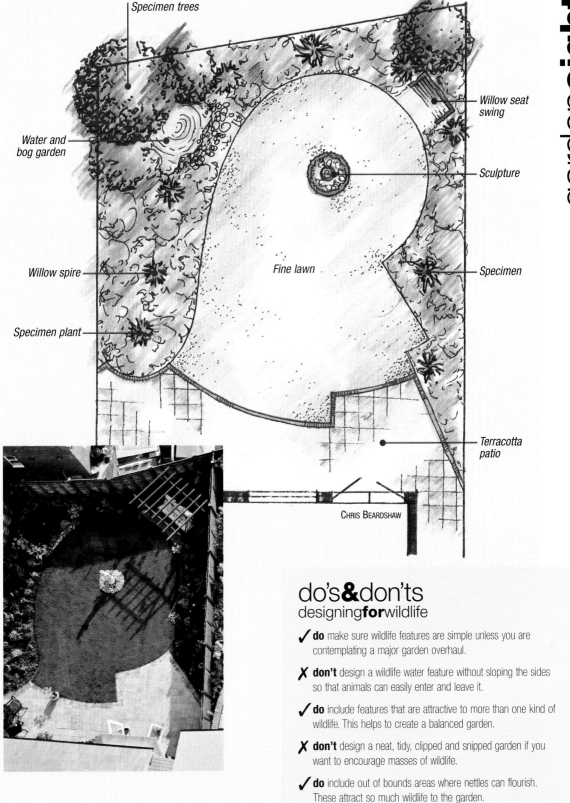

Specimen trees

Willow seat swing

Water and bog garden

Sculpture

Willow spire

Fine lawn

Specimen

Specimen plant

Terracotta patio

CHRIS BEARDSHAW

do's&don'ts
designing**for**wildlife

✓ **do** make sure wildlife features are simple unless you are contemplating a major garden overhaul.

✗ **don't** design a wildlife water feature without sloping the sides so that animals can easily enter and leave it.

✓ **do** include features that are attractive to more than one kind of wildlife. This helps to create a balanced garden.

✗ **don't** design a neat, tidy, clipped and snipped garden if you want to encourage masses of wildlife.

✓ **do** include out of bounds areas where nettles can flourish. These attract so much wildlife to the garden.

makingamosaic

The gorgeous mosaic in Garden 5 is simple yet stunning and brought together colour, shape, texture, personality and practical skills. Traditionally, mosaics are made from glass, ceramics or cobbles and were used extensively by the Romans in their not so humble abodes.

Ali created a circular area in the corner of the garden. A section of the existing curved wall formed the outer perimeter of the feature, and an additional low brick wall was built to complete a circle. However, whatever the site and shape of a mosaic, the basic method of making one is the same.

1 Make a pad of concrete and allow it to set solid. As with all garden floorings, the pad must be built on a slight gradient to prevent water forming puddles.

2 Once the concrete is solid, or cured, mark a design on the surface. This involves lots of sketching, masses of detailed drawing and plenty of running upstairs to a high window for a better view. It is impossible to walk to an area and draw the design without standing back. So stand back, and stand as high as possible. Then the fun begins.

3 Arm yourself with bags of tiles, all sorted according to colour and shape. In Garden 5 small ceramic tiles were used to create the pattern: sheets of these are available from builders' merchants, and individual tiles are snipped off with tile cutters. Square tiles, all different shades of blue, were perfect for most of

the mosaic and pieces of broken tile were used to fill in gaps where the design dictated.

4 Place a thin layer of mortar on a small section of the design. Then, with infinite patience, press the tiles into the mortar, following the design, and allow the mortar to set. Only mix small amounts of mortar at any one time to prevent it hardening before the tiles are pressed into place.

5 You can use spacers to ensure even spacing of the tiles on geometric designs. However, the mosaic in Garden 5 is one case where a little bit of guesswork resulted in a more authentic look.

6 Continue the process until the mosaic is complete. You would have to be a speedy worker to finish a large design in a single day,

so, if necessary, cover it at night to protect it from rain which would prevent the mortar from setting hard.

7 When the design is complete – and only then – put mortar between the tiles. The gaps should be large enough to allow you to place, or point, it between the tiles. Take care not to put mortar on the tile surface – wipe it off if you do. Leave until everything is dry.

8 Finally, polish up the tiles with a dry cloth for a sparkling conclusion.

In Garden 5 a seating area was constructed around the mosaic to allow visitors to admire the result of weeks of work and artistry. The only limit to a design is your imagination.

styleorvile?

It is dangerous to say that any one aspect of gardening is trendy, à la mode, in vogue. It is equally daring to say that any plant, feature or type of flooring is nasty, crass, outdated and definitely not for today's gardeners. Trends come and go in gardening, as with all other aspects of life, but sometimes it seems that when something becomes popular it instantly becomes unfashionable.

The gardening neighbours are delighted with their gardens, but the observant among you may have noticed some controversial additions and absentees from the gardens. Garden gnomes appeared very late on in the design for Garden 8. They are a family tradition, and wherever their owners go they follow. Quirky and fun – what's wrong with that? Where is the practical, maintenance-free plastic-resin furniture? Can millions of users be wrong? Pampas grass is nowhere to be seen and for some reason carries a naff stigma. Is there a more impressive flowering plant for October?

Ferns, a Victorian favourite, were relegated to the textbooks but their popularity revived a few years ago – a great example to pampas grass and also to *Lavatera* or mallow, another much maligned, easy to grow, floriferous plant that is currently out of favour. Leylandii conifers may never recover from the battering of their bad press coverage, but in the right place and in the right hands they surely have a place in someone's garden?

Decking came from the United States and Scandinavia to a miserable fanfare that could only be heard around the wooden piers of seaside resorts. Now everyone is embracing and nailing down decking boards. But is its popularity going to fade in the face of competition from gravel, ground-glass beads and stainless steel? Time will tell. Brightly coloured painted fences and structures lighten many gardens, but are too much blue paint, plants and furnishings used today? Results in the *Gardening Neighbours* gardens say blue is here to stay.

Whatever your thoughts, your garden is exactly that: your garden. Do in it whatever you please, and please yourself.

construction

construct *v.* to put together substances or parts systematically; build; assemble.

Constructing the framework, the skeleton, the outline of a garden is easier than you think. Chris and Ali's designs for *Gardening Neighbours* included lots of construction in every one of the plots, and for good reasons. The ups, sides and downs of a garden combine to frame the complete picture. The downs also provide essential walkways to different features and the ups and sides offer support to plants.

Paths are the practical way to get around a garden and link features, focal points, compost bins and the way out. They can be made of anything from bricks, concrete slabs or bark chippings to a regularly mown area through a wildife lawn.

All the construction work has to look good, and to ensure it stays looking terrific for decades the time spent on planning is vital. It is tempting to launch into a project, full of enthusiasm, without marking out, measuring up and ordering everything you will need to finish the job. It may be tempting, but resist the temptation. Concrete will continue to set as you race down to the builders' merchant for a couple of missing bricks. Get it right from the start, and construction in the garden will be fun and fulfilling.

going**up**

pergolas

Pergolas are used in two of the *Gardening Neighbours* gardens. The one in Garden 8 is free-standing and the other, in Garden 1, is fixed to the house wall. The main consideration when constructing either type is headroom. Anything less than 2m (6ft 6in) will cause headaches for taller visitors.

Free-standing pergolas: The free-standing pergola in Garden 8 frames the seating area and allows plants to hang and climb. It also creates valuable shade in the south-facing plot. It uses the traditionally forgotten vertical space of the garden and adds a mature feel to the design.

Free-standing pergolas require supports at each corner in the form of stout wooden posts, and are easy to construct. Kits are available, making siting the structure the hardest part of the operation.

(above) Place a driving tool in the fixing post before hammering into the soil.

(right) Space cross-beams or rafters equally for a superb finish.

(far right) Mortise joints ensure a solid structure.

Supporting posts must be firmly embedded in the ground, and there are two main methods of ensuring that, once erected, your pergola stays upright.

The first involves using metal spikes, bought separately from pergola kits, that are driven into the soil. Each post then slots into the top of a spike, and is tightened using the bolts provided. This is the easy, non-messy way but success depends on getting the spikes into the soil vertically. Any deviation will result in your post sticking out at a strange angle, not exactly conducive to great garden design. It is therefore helpful to have someone to hold the base of the spike firmly in the soil as you strike the top with a lump hammer. Metal spikes are great if you intend to move the pergola to a new home or ever need to replace the posts. Simply unbolt, renew and tighten up.

The second way of securing the posts in the soil is setting them in concrete. Dig holes 60cm (2ft) deep and wide to accommodate each post. Once the structure is finalized, drop the posts into the holes and pack them in with a concrete mix consisting of 5 parts ballast to 1 part cement. If you

are only constructing one pergola and don't require masses of concrete, bags of ready-mixed post-setting concrete are available from builders' merchants. All you need do is pour the dry mix into the hole around the base of each post and add water. The mix then sets in hours. Your own mixed concrete will set overnight.

Lean-to pergolas: In Garden 1 the lean-to pergola extends the house into the garden and provides a walkway along its length which will be dripping in plants and flowers. It requires upright supports along one length, and relies on a wooden wall plate fixed to the house wall for support down the other length. The upright supports are set in concrete or metal spikes as for the free-standing pergola. When you are constructing a lean-to pergola the angle of the roofline is important to the finished look of the structure. Bearing in mind the headroom measurement, the wall plate should be fixed somewhere below the first-floor window sills. Final measurements depend on individual designs.

The wall plate is securely bolted to the wall using anchor bolts. The rafters of the pergola are fixed to the wall plate either by slotting them into a mortise joint – a chunk cut out of the wood that allows two pieces of wood to fit snugly together – or with screws. A mortise joint is stronger than screws. Rafters are usually spaced 1m (3ft) apart, but this depends on the design of your pergola.

Metal hanging brackets that fix rafters to a wall instead of to a wall plate are available from builders' merchants. The rafters slot into the brackets and nails or screws fixed through the sides of the brackets secure them and prevent them popping out.

(opposite) In Garden 1 a pergola runs along the length of the house.

(top right) Archways in Garden 7 frame the garden and lead the eye around the garden.

(right) Simple joints result in a solid archway capable of supporting plant growth.

archways

In Garden 7 metal archways were used to frame a walkway around the perimeter of the lawn area. They also provide support for clematis and fruit trees. An archway is easily erected by first pushing the anchorage points into the soil, or, for extra safety, cementing them into the ground, as you would for fence posts. It is then assembled by slotting and bolting the pieces together. Plants are tied to the structure using plant ties, twine or wire. Rustic-style archways are similar in construction and, again, only need to be bolted together and made secure.

going**sideways**

fencing

Given an extra pair of hands, strong gloves all round and a still day, fencing is easy. Set up the first fencing post using one of the methods described for pergolas. If you're using metal spikes you can proceed quickly along the complete length of the fencing as you don't have to wait for concrete to set.

Erect the posts and panels alternately, using wooden battens to support posts set in concrete.

Regularly check levels throughout the project as hammering nails into posts may jolt them away from the vertical: offer a panel up to a post and check that the top of the panel is horizontal before securing it to the post with nails. Use galvanized nails as these will not rust or create run marks down the posts. Drive the nails in at an angle, through the edge of the panel into the post. Alternatively, use fence-post clips. These are nailed to the post and the panel slots into the clip. Nails are driven through the sides of the clip into the post. Clips are helpful if the panel frames are thin and easily split.

Panels can also be slotted into grooves in concrete posts which makes nailing unnecessary. If rattling occurs in windy weather pack small pieces of wood into the offending gaps.

Garden 8 has wattle fencing all around its perimeter, and it looks sensational. Strips of flexible branches, usually hazel or willow, are woven horizontally around sturdy poles. These can then be erected in the usual fence-panel way, or simply used as decoration in front of plain panels. The fencing provides a cottage-garden atmosphere and suits the garden down to the ground.

setting**posts**in**the**ground

Whether you are constructing a pergola or a fence, if you are setting posts in the ground here are a few guidelines to ensure your feature's longevity and success.

● Although all timber that will be below ground level has to be tanalized – pressure-treated with chemicals to stop it rotting – you can preserve your posts further by standing them in large buckets of preservative for two days before setting them in the soil. Then wrap the portion that will be underground in polythene bags before sinking them into the hole. On heavy clay soils, place the base of the post on a layer of grit to help water drain away from it.

Ensure fence panels and decorative panels are level, well supported or fixed.

how**deep**?

For stable, upright posts that remain stable and upright for decades, a portion has to be buried in the soil.

60cm (2ft) above ground needs 25cm (10in) below ground.

90cm (3ft) above ground needs 30cm (12in) below ground.

120cm (4ft) above ground needs 45cm (18in) below ground.

150cm (5ft) above ground needs 60cm (24in) below ground.

180cm (6ft) above ground needs 90cm (36in) below ground.

A 180cm (6ft) fencing panel will therefore require a post 270cm (9ft) high. This may be stating the obvious, but too many people discover that in their enthusiasm they have overlooked this simple calculation.

sloping**gardens**

The trick to fencing on a slope is to create terraces or panels of equal heights that descend down the length of the garden. The drop between each section is the same, ensuring a 'professional' look. This avoids sloping the panels along the fence length. Fill the gaps below the panels with concrete gravel boards, available from garden retailers.

- When the post is in its hole, pack broken bricks around its base. Ideally, it should stand up upright without the help of concrete.
- When you add the concrete pack it in hard between the bricks and around the base of the post. This will enable the post to withstand wind and people bumping into it. Another polythene bag over the top of the concrete will help it to set hard. Concrete will start doing its job after three days, but will take a month to be at full strength.
- When concreting the post, shape the concrete at its base so that water flows away from the wood. This reduces the chances of rotting.
- Check the level of posts throughout the concreting process and adjust as necessary. Support them by nailing battens to each side once concreting has been completed by ramming the non-nailed end of the batten into the surrounding soil. Battens are removed once the concrete has set.

- Metal post supports save time on mixing concrete and are great if your ground is soft. Position the spike on the soil and drive it down using a lump hammer or sledgehammer. Bashing it directly on its top may cause damage so put a driving tool, sometimes called a dolly, into the top of the support. This will withstand, but won't impede, your efforts. Good driving tools have small handles at the sides that allow you to make slight adjustments to the angle of the post. Remember, the supports must be vertical if the post is to look good. Metal supports for securing posts into concrete slabs, stone or driveways are available. These bolt into the hard surface and the post slots and tightens into the top of the support.
- Always fix a capping to every post. This stops water from settling, then seeping into the wood to cause rotting. Plastic or wooden caps are available from garden retailers.

going**down**

gravel**and**pebbles

Gravel and pebbles are used in many *Gardening Neighbours* gardens to create fantastic flooring. They instantly lighten and show off dark-leafed plants to perfection. They are also simplicity itself to put down. 'Gravel is a great design material,' Ali Ward says. 'It is available in so many colours and textures, you can find gravel to suit any style of garden. We used honey-coloured small gravel through pebbles to large boulders for dressing. Accurate levelling of the soil isn't necessary as gravel and pebbles even out mounds and hollows.

Remove all stones, sticks and weeds from the surface of the soil and roll out a planting membrane. This allows water to move down through the soil but stops weeds from growing up. Then it's a case of filling your wheelbarrow, wheeling it into position and tipping out the gravel or pebbles. Rake the surface level and stand back. Planting is easy. Just push the flooring aside, cut the planting membrane, insert the plant and plant it into a hole. Then fold the membrane back and gently arrange the pebbles or gravel around the base of the plant.

> **'Gravel requires no maintenance other than the occasional rake'**
> *Ali Ward*

This type of flooring also protects the soil and tender roots in freezing weather and can act as tiny storage heaters around plants, absorbing heat during the day and releasing it at night. Weeds have trouble rooting, as historically seeds falling on stony ground have tended to fail. Pebbles and gravel are both available in small bags for topping up, or dressing the surface of compost in pots and containers. Larger loads can be bought from builders' merchants and delivered to your front door. It is advisable to cover the ground with a thick plastic sheet if you are expecting a delivery as it is difficult to remove scratches and scuff marks from dark surfaces.

decking

Wooden decking is used to great effect in the *Gardening Neighbours* gardens. Once seen only in the United States and Scandinavia, it is now the first flooring material many gardeners think of, and for good reasons. It's versatile, easy to work with, the results are spectacular and the wood complements the rest of the garden. For impressive examples of how innovative design and the choice of wood dovetail, check out the *Gardening Neighbours* gardens. The decking in Garden 4 looks superb and is totally functional, used for the walkway from the house and the circular sitting area. In Garden 1 the decking leads the owner from the house into the sitting area around a water feature.

> **'The use of decking in garden design is not a new idea. There were wooden, tiered steps in the original private gardens at Hampton Court'**
> *Ali Ward*

If you put wooden decking directly on the soil it will never provide a flat surface. It is therefore held above ground level on a wooden framework, identical to the wooden floorboards in many houses. The trick is to produce a solid, level framework that is capable of supporting the decking, furniture and visitors without any bowing or bending. Preparation is the key to becoming a decking devotee.

Constructing a deck: Support is needed around the perimeter of a deck, and evenly spaced mini-foundations are required.

1 Every 1.5m (5ft) around the perimeter of your proposed deck dig out a hole 30cm (12in) deep and square, and fill it with concrete. After this has hardened build up the foundation to the desired level with bricks and mortar.

2 Place an outer framework of timber on the foundations. The joists, running at an angle of 90° to the decking, will be nailed to this. Position the joists at 45cm (18in) intervals to provide enough support for the decking.

Hire a sander to smooth decking before staining or painting.

do's&don'ts

✓ **do** ensure that the soil or ground beneath the decking is level before starting out on the project.

✗ **don't** skimp on the foundations and joists; these stop the deck wobbling and/or bending.

✓ **do** place the decking boards loosely on the joists and framework to check that your measurements and quantities are correct.

✗ **don't** guess at the size of gaps between boards; use spacers for a professional look.

✓ **do** ensure that all nails, or screws, are below the surface of the decking boards to prevent snagging.

✗ **don't** paint, or add preservative to, dirty, unsanded decking. Sand and sweep to produce a smooth finish.

✓ **do** use spare boards as fascias to complete the look.

3 Before jumping to the nice part – nailing the decking boards – check that the framework and joists are solid. Walk all over the joists and if you feel any movement of the timber, pack gaps between joists and soil with wood, bricks or stones. The framework must be solid before you continue.

4 Place the decking boards at right angles to the joists. If you are confident that your calculations are correct, get nailing straightaway. However, it is better to place the decking boards on the framework and check that you have enough of them, and that the proposed gap between each board results in the final board being flush with the outer framework, eliminating the need to cut a board along its length. This saves time and effort, and looks better.

5 Once you are happy, get nailing. If the decking adjoins your house and protrudes into the garden start nailing at the house end, moving towards the garden. Nail through the decking boards into the joists below, using two nails per position. Once the first length of decking is nailed in place, you will have to finalize the gap between it and the next, and the next, and the next, and so on. Consistently spaced boards look terrific, whereas ones that are inconsis-

tently spaced look poor. The gap itself can be as wide as you want, but make it too small and water may not run off the surface, too big and your foot could disappear between the boards. You will already have an idea of the size of the gaps because you placed all the boards on the framework before you started nailing.

Make spacers to the desired gap-size from offcuts, and place these between subsequent boards as you proceed with the project. As a quick guide, the head of a 5cm (2in) flat-headed nail, when dropped pointed end down between the gaps between boards, is an ideal spacing.

6 Before packing your hammer away for the day, remove all spacers and check that all nails are hammered flush with the boards.

Screws are an alternative to nails. They don't pop up with time and produce a deck that can easily be removed, for example if you are moving house and garden. However, they are more time-consuming. If you use screws, ensure that they are countersunk below the surface of the boards.

7 When all the boards are nailed in place, the decking may need sanding down before you apply any topcoats of preservatives or lacquer. A hired belt-sander is perfect for the job. Sand the

boards down as often as time allows to produce a smooth finish to the decking.

8 Finally, nail fascia boards around the edge of the deck. Use spare boards to match the decking surface.

Decking extras: Using coloured decking is a quick way to completely transform the look of a garden, and boards prestained in a variety of colours are available from DIY stores and timber merchants. However, unless you are 100 per cent sure of your colour scheme and design, buy natural-coloured wood, construct your deck and live with it for a few weeks before getting the colour charts out.

A large expanse of brightly coloured decking would detract from the pebbles, gorgeous pots and planting in Garden 4, so it is staying natural blonde. In Garden 8 a brown preservative was used for the decking as well as for the pergola and swinging seat as dirty gardening boots would make a mess of light-coloured boards.

Grooved boards are available and are not as slippery as smooth ones in wet weather. It is also possible to buy decking that looks like a row of cobbles or brickwork. It is great in the wet and looks wonderful into the bargain.

gardeningneighbours

Garden 1 has low-level decking whose boards converge on a focal point beyond the centrally located water feature. It looks superb, but cutting each board along its length was time-consuming. Calculating how much to taper each board also took some time, but the work involved in producing this subtlety paid off.

The decking in Garden 4 is held higher than normal, with a walkway meeting a circular seating and leisure area. The joists are bolted to thick wooden posts buried 60cm (2ft) in the ground.

All the wood used in the *Gardening Neighbours* gardens is pressure-treated to ensure longevity.

Preservative is forced to the centre of wood during tanalizing. This ensures longevity of wood and structures.

buyingwood

Kits for decking, pergolas and fences are usually of excellent quality. Because of the destruction of hardwood rainforests, most wood used in garden construction is now softwood. This comes from managed pine forests and looks good, but will rot in time if used untreated. Manufacturers tanalize or pressure-treat wood to ensure that the entire thickness of a post or plank is saturated with chemical preservatives. Quality wood will last for decades — the decking used in Garden 4 is Southern Yellow Pine and has been so well treated that it carries a twenty-five-year guarantee. The preservative can be seen at the heart of the upright decking posts.

Looking at a cut end of timber will reveal how far in the preservative has been forced. A thin outer layer is useless — look for colour at the centre. For a belt-and-braces approach to the wood in your garden add your own layer of preservative. Check for, and reject, timber that is cracked, split or has large knotholes. Also reject any wood that is warped as it will never straighten to produce an upright pergola or fence post.

paving

It may be a path, it could be a patio, or it might be a driveway, but paving in one of its various guises will be employed somewhere in your garden. The wide choice of materials can be overwhelming. First decide on the kind of traffic your paving is going to be subjected to. A surface that has a car trundling up and down on it will need a very different material to one that has to put up with nothing more than an occasional stroll to a retractable washing line. Concrete slabs are the usual choice for patios, and many colours and textures are available from garden retailers. Bricks and blocks are great for driveways and, because they are small, are wonderful for creating intricate patterns. Large slabs of stone or concrete may cover more of the ground at one go, but they are heavier to lift than smaller versions.

Think carefully about your design before choosing a material, as once it is laid it is difficult to lift. Beautiful tiles from Europe are used in Garden 3 to create a Mediterranean feel. They are small and do not dominate, but add so much to the design. The gentle terracotta colour slides to pink as dusk nestles around the garden. Illuminated by low-voltage lights, the tiles add atmosphere to what is potentially a cold, stark surface.

As with all construction work in the *Gardening Neighbours* gardens, the success is in the preparation, and with paving that means foundations. A patio used for drinks at seven and barbecues at midnight only requires foundations to be 10cm (4in) deep. However, the driveway catering for all your guests' cars will need double that depth.

Constructing a stone slab pathway or patio:

1 Dig a trench for a pathway or excavate the shape of your proposed patio.

2 Nail straight pieces of timber together and use these as temporary walls around the perimeter of your construction. They will retain the sand, ballast and mortar.

3 Firm and level the soil and add a 5cm (2in) layer of hard core or broken bricks.

4 Spread ballast, available from builders' merchants, all over the hard-core surface to fill the holes between the larger stones or bricks. Ram this layer down as it will be the one that supports the slabs or bricks, evenly distributing their weight over its surface.

5 Place a 5cm (2in) layer of sharp sand on the hard core, and ensure it is pressed down and levelled.

6 Place all the slabs you will be using on top of the sand and check that spaces are even. Use offcuts of wood as spacers.

7 Lift the first slab and place five blobs of mortar, one at each corner and one in the middle of where the slab will rest, directly on the sand. Replace the slab, and use a block of wood and a rubber mallet to firm it onto the mortar.

8 Do the same for all the slabs, checking the slope is consistent and gaps are equal.

9 After a couple of days brush a dry mortar-mix of sand and cement into the joints.

sticky**stones**

Garden 6 has an unusual yet ingenious covering for its hard surfaces. A layer of fine stones is stuck onto a mastic glue to produce a hard-wearing surface that looks terrific. Kits are available from builders' merchants.

sloping**patios**

- Always slope patios away from the house to avoid water damage to brickwork.

- Ensure the slope is consistent along the length of the patio (or driveway or path) to avoid a puddle forming during rainy weather.

- If you are butting a patio directly against a house wall make sure it is at least 15cm (6in) below the damp-proof course. Never cover airbricks: cutting holes in the patio is preferable to blocking vital airflow.

Brick or paviour surfaces: When laying a brick or paviour surface don't bother to slap blobs of mortar on the sharp sand. The bricks are best firmed directly into it. More sand is then brushed between the joints to bind the bricks together. Ideally, you will use a plate vibrator to bed all the bricks into the sand and help it work its way deep between the joints. These vibrators are available from tool-hire companies, but if you can't hire one place a large piece of wood on the bricks or paviours and bash it with a rubber mallet. This settles them nicely. Walking on the surface will highlight any wobbly, insecure individuals in need of attention. Lift, add or remove sharp sand as necessary, and replace the bricks or paviours.

boundary**edges**

Edges prevent paths, patios, driveways and lawns from spreading or crumbling. There is, as there seems to be in every aspect of gardening, a vast choice of materials. The gardening neighbours favoured bricks placed on their edges, or laid soldier fashion. These were used in most of the gardens and constituted the boundary between patio and lawn. They were also used as a finishing touch in the construction of walling. Place the bricks on their edges, on a bed of mortar, and fill or point the gaps between them with even more mortar. This gives a solid bound-

ary to whatever material you use for your pathway or patio.

The alternative to brick edging is to use a thin wooden rail. If all your borders or paths are straight it is simply a matter of digging a trench and fixing the timber to pegs driven into the soil. The rail is low and is usually positioned at the same level as the patio, path or lawn. Positioning it slightly below the surface of a lawn enables you to mow straight up to the edge without blunting the blades on your mower. If the rail, or any edging material, sticks up higher than the lawn edge you will need to cut the straggly edges of your lawn carefully with shears or a line trimmer.

If your path or lawn is curved there is a simple trick to make the wood bend without snapping. Saw notches at 15cm (6in) intervals along the entire length of the rail. These will give it some flexibility, usually enough to curve gently around bends.

Formal-looking edging tiles were popular in Victorian gardens and still look great today. Mark out a line with taut string and dig a trench

Bricks laid on their edges act as a solid barrier to soil slip or movement of slabs. Place on a bed of mortar and firm down with a rubber mallet.

two-thirds the depth of the tile. Place the tile in the trench, firm the soil around it and you have a perfect Victorian boundary edge. Check out antique shops for authentic tiles or trawl builders' merchants for impressive copies.

steps

Before Chris and Ali got moving on the designs, all the *Gardening Neighbours* plots were flat. The simple use of steps creates stimulating changes in level, increasing the interest of a garden.

Steps are easy to build if the slope is gentle. Put a firm mix of mortar on the compacted soil and lay a concrete slab on top. Add a thicker layer of mortar and place another slab on top of this to take your first steps. Repeat until you have stepped the desired area.

On steeper slopes cut a terrace of steps in the soil, place a layer of mortar on top of each terrace and lay the concrete slabs on the mortar.

On even steeper slopes, or as in the case of the gardening neighbours where a giant leap for garden kind was required, small retaining walls are needed. Dig out terraces and then build a small wall, perhaps two bricks high, at the front of each one. Once the mortar has set solid in the mini-walls, backfill with more mortar, firming the mortar solidly into place. This produces a solid wall. Lay slabs on top to finish the steps. To maintain an even and professional look ensure that each step, or riser, is the same height. Let the whole construction set before treading on the steps.

Step guide: Steps must be functional, and their size is critical for comfortable use. Try to make yours at least 75cm (2ft 6in) wide – a width of 120cm (4ft) is preferable if you expect busy open-garden days. To avoid the need for small ladders, make the height or riser of each step around 15cm (6in). Ideally, steps should be 45cm (18in) deep with a fall of 1cm (½in) from back to front to help drainage. Overhanging the tread of a step over the one below will help to prevent tripping.

concrete**and**mortar

When you are constructing features in your garden you will not be able to avoid concrete and mortar. Concrete is used to make foundations for summer houses and for setting fence and pergola posts. It is made by mixing cement, aggregates and water. Mortar is used to stick slabs and bricks to each other and is made by mixing cement and building sand. A plasticizer is often used to make it more workable, and colouring can be added if a close match to existing mortar is required.

> **'I would use any material at any point if I felt it was appropriate for the location and the best material for creating the atmosphere I was after'**
> *Chris Beardshaw*

Most builders' merchants have different grades of sand, graded according to the size of the particles. Builder's or soft sand has a small range of particle sizes, generally the smallest of all sands, and is used to make mortar. Sharp sand has a wide range of particle sizes and is used for concrete. Silver sand, which is also used when making concrete, has particles of all sizes.

Applying rendering or concrete to walls helps to prevent damage by moisture.

- When mixing concrete and mortar, combine the dry ingredients to form an evenly coloured mix. Pile this up and make a small crater in the top. Pour a little water into the crater, mixing all the time, and keep sprinkling on more water, little by little, until the mixture is the desired consistency.
- A quick consistency check for concrete is to smooth out the pile with the back of your shovel. The surface should remain moist without breaking up or forming a layer of water.
- A quick consistency check for mortar is to push a trowel into the mix. The mix is ready for action if the impression of the tool remains and doesn't fill with water or crumble.
- If you are working with concrete or mortar on a hot day, cover the wet mixes with a polythene sheet to stop them setting hard too quickly.
- Always clean mixing tools immediately after use to avoid staining.

cleaning**tips**

All the structures in the *Gardening Neighbours* gardens are easy to clean and maintain. The slate in Garden 3 is washed with running water and brushed clean, and isn't susceptible to moss or algae growth.

The walls in most of the gardens are rendered and only require washing with clean water or, if moss grows in future years, with a moss cleaner.

The exposed brick in Garden 5 may become covered with a fluffy white deposit called efflorescence. If you have a similar wall and this happens to you, there is no need to lose confidence in yourself or your builder. The deposits are only salts being drawn from the brick. Remove them with a scrubbing brush — but don't use water as this will only encourage more salts to be released. Cement stains on brickwork fade with time, but care throughout construction work is vital.

painting**tips**

Gardening Neighbours utilized fantastic paint colours in all the gardens. Here are some guidelines to follow.

- Never use gloss paint. The airtight seal traps moisture below the surface and when the water evaporates it causes bubbles and blisters. Instead use paints and stains specially formulated for outdoor use on wood and walls. They allow water to escape and the wood to breathe.

- Always read the instructions. Some products need stirring to ensure a consistent colour throughout use, while all that others require is that the lid is taken off and a brush is plunged in.

- Be prepared to apply more than one coat to new, dry wood. Alternatively, if you want a washed effect read the instructions to check dilution rates.

- Always sand down wood to ensure a smooth finish.

safety**first**

- Never leap out of bed and dive straight into heavy lifting and lugging. If you do, chances are you will strain a few muscles and put your project back by weeks. Warm up before you move that just-delivered hundredweight of bricks by doing some gentle stretching.

- Always wear appropriate safety clothing – gloves when you're handling cement, eye-protectors when cutting stone and timber, and protective boots when doing anything in the garden.

- Ensure all tools are kept away from prying and inquisitive fingers and always connect electrical ones to a residual current device. It may save lives.

- Never rush a project just to finish it before daylight disappears. Let it run over to the next day and get it right, the safe way.

tools**of**the**trade**

Hiring tools is a great way to produce fantastic results without massive financial outlay on equipment that will only be used once or twice.

- A cement mixer is the tool for mixing a large quantity of concrete.

- Using a belt-sander is the best way to sand down even a small area of decking.

- Powered nail guns and jigsaws make light work of large decking projects.

- Giant corkscrews, called post-hole borers, twist into the ground and remove cores of soil. Great if you are erecting a long stretch of fencing that requires lots of posts.

- Use plate vibrators to firm bricks or paviours into the underlying bed of sand. They ensure a solid finish to a path or patio.

- An extra pair of helpful hands is essential with most construction work.

chapterthree

water features

water *n.* a clear colourless tasteless odourless liquid that is essential for plant and animal life and constitutes, in impure form, rain, oceans, rivers, lakes etc.

feature *n.* a prominent or distinctive part, as of a landscape, book etc.

adding water to a garden brings it to life, and in *Gardening Neighbours* Chris and Ali injected vitality into what were previously barren plots. Being a natural element, water fits seamlessly into garden designs and can be either still or sparkling. The natural-look pond in Garden 8 is an easy water feature to place in a design and construct in a garden. Its relative stillness attracts wildlife and ushers in a feeling of calm, peace and tranquillity. Sparkling water can be anything from the bubbling stream in Garden 2 to a full frontal assault on the senses with exciting waterfalls cascading, tumbling and thundering from varying heights, all possible in Garden 1. Most gardeners restrain this Niagara effect and create features that look fantastic, sound relaxing and fuse the different elements of design into a complete unit, a unit of total garden.

These features can be for everyone and their gardens. The gardening neighbours had space to develop ideas for theirs, but smaller areas can still include water. 'If the water, in whatever guise, enhances the space in a way that cannot be achieved by anything else then it is worth including,' says Chris Beardshaw. You don't even need a garden to be creative as there are no limits when considering a water feature.

simply**speaking**

A sparkling-water feature is a reservoir of water that is recycled by a pump. The water can travel a short or long distance along a lined route, but it ultimately arrives back where it started. The rest is artistic decoration. A still-water feature is a reservoir of water without a pump. Water features can be that simple.

The four main components of a water feature are water, reservoir, liner and pump.

water
Tap water is always used. It is safe for plants and fish if it is allowed to stand for three days to allow any chlorine present to evaporate. Rain will add small amounts of water to features, but tap water should be used for topping up.

reservoir
This is usually a large plastic container that acts as a sump. It must be watertight and large enough to supply the water requirements of the feature. It also has to withstand losses due to evaporation and drifting spray. Build a large reservoir into your design as it is annoying and time-consuming to top up a water feature every day. For mini, self-contained, fountains the reservoir is directly below the fountain nozzle. In features where the water moves along to form a stream, as in Gardens 2 and 3, a large reservoir is positioned at the lowest point of the stream.

> '**It's a myth that water is an expensive and troublesome element to include in the garden**'
> *Chris Beardshaw*

liners
An option that is open to anyone with heavy clay soil like that in the *Gardening Neighbours* gardens is to wet the soil, allow it to bake hard in the sun, and repeat the process a few times to produce a rock-hard, impermeable surface. It's

Metal grids placed over reservoirs ensure that dirt, people and animals stay out.
Make sure grids are strong enough to withstand the weight of any features placed on top.

Line reservoirs, pumps or features with butyl lining. Mould the lining to the shape of the hole before trickling water in.

not always successful, and buying a liner is easier and more effective. Two main types of liner are available to gardeners: rigid, preformed liners and flexible liners.

Rigid, preformed liners: These range in size from complete fountain units a metre in diameter to the ubiquitous kidney-shaped affairs.

1 Place the liner on the soil and mark out the shape, adding 30cm (12in) to the outline. Excavate the soil to make a hole 10cm (4in) deeper than the depth of the liner.

2 Compact the soil in the base of the hole and add a 10cm (4in) layer of sand.

3 Carefully lower the liner and fit it into the hole. Use planks of straight wood and a spirit level to check that the liner is level. If it isn't, and don't be surprised if this is the case, take the liner out and add or remove sand as necessary.

4 Once everything is level, start trickling water into the liner using a hosepipe. While this is happening, start filling in the gap around the liner with soil that has been sieved – stones have to be removed as they can puncture all types of liner. Firm this soil with your foot as the water trickles into the liner.

5 Fit your pump and start the nice part – decorating to fit your design.

Flexible liners: Flexible liners allow you to make a feature in any size or shape, such as the gardening neighbours' running streams. They are also used to line above-ground concrete, wooden, stone or brick water features. Black polythene and PVC are both unsuitable for long-term use. They are not strong enough to withstand heavy wear and tear, split easily and become brittle if exposed to sunlight. Butyl rubber liner was the choice of the gardening neighbours as it is thin, supple, easy to work with and withstands small movements of underlying soil over years of service. Initially it is more expensive than other types of liner, but it will not need replacing for at least twenty years. Butyl liner is resistant to ultraviolet light, cold, roots and tears. A handy product when designing and constructing water features – and fitting is easy.

1 Mark out the desired shape of the water feature and excavate the soil as for rigid liners. Check the sides are level using the plank and spirit level technique. Remove all sticks and stones and cover the surface of the hole or stream

hard**sums**

Butyl liner is sold in fixed widths, but by the running metre or yard. You could guess how much you will need, but it will be costly if you underestimate and need to overlap and seal. Equally, overestimating will cost a fortune and you'll have metres of unwanted butyl. Calculating how much liner you require is easy.

- Measure the length, the maximum depth and the widest part of your water feature, in metres.

- Double the depth measurement and add it to the length measurement (A).

- Double the depth measurement again and add it to the width measurement (B).

- Multiply the two figures (A x B) to get the area of your water feature in square metres.

Take this figure to a butyl-liner retailer and let them cut the correct size. The retailer will add a little bit, possibly 45cm (18in), to allow for tucks, folds and miscalculations.

with 5cm (2in) of wet sand. An alternative to sand is a non-woven fabric liner, similar to carpet underlay, which stops stones and sharp objects piercing the butyl. Simply cut the fabric and place it on the soil before laying out the butyl liner. Leave the butyl liner in the sun for a couple of hours as this improves its flexibility.

2 Place the liner over the hole or stream and gently fill it with water, ensuring that any tucks and folds are smoothed out. Once the liner is filled and settled trim its edges, allowing 15cm (6in) overlap around the top of the hole.

3 Fit your pump and start the nice part – decorating.

If are using a butyl liner for an above-ground structure like the impressive fountain in Garden 1, warm the butyl in the sun, place it in the structure and gently fill it with water. Again, have an overlap around the top. This will be covered with edging materials once the liner has completely settled.

pumps

There is a bewildering choice of pumps but they all belong to one of three groups.

Surface pumps: Surface pumps are installed near a water feature, in a well-ventilated protective unit like a shed. They are only used for large-scale features such as the streams in Gardens 2 and 3.

Submersible pumps: Submersible pumps are ideal for all water features. All you need to do is connect and place the pump in the feature and plug it in. Ensure that it is raised slightly off the bottom of the feature or reservoir by placing it on a brick, an upturned pond plant basket or a specially manufactured platform. This will stop the pump sucking in all the sludge at the bottom of the feature and clogging the filters. It may be necessary to fix small pumps, often used for

The powerful pump with integral lights in garden 1 is also remote-controlled.

pebble pools, to the support as they are light-weight and may move in the water. The pump then does what a pump does, and that's pump. It may pump water up through a nozzle to create a fine spray of water, or it may return water to the start of a stream or wall-mounted feature.

Solar-powered pumps: If you find the thought of electricity in the garden scary, consider using a solar-powered pump. Solar panels gather the sun's rays and convert them into electricity to run the pump. There are obvious drawbacks, the main one being the loss of power on a dull day. They are also unable to produce enough power to drive medium-sized water features. Solar pumps are good for pebble pools in places that mains electricity cannot reach.

pump-**buying**know-**how**

A session with a knowledgeable pump retailer will sort out your requirements. However, it will be both helpful and time-saving to know the answers to some of the questions that will be fired your way.

- The size of the water feature is essential in selecting the correct pump.
- Its capacity, in litres, is also important.
- How high you want to pump the water if you are planning a waterfall or fountain is crucial.
- You will also be asked about flow rates. This is the amount of water that flows through a pump in any given hour and is a guide to the capabilities of a particular pump. Powerful, adaptable ones have higher flow-rate figures. The flow rate is, of course, linked to the capacity of your water feature. A rough guide is that it should never be more than half of the volume of your water feature. In other words, make sure there is plenty of water in reserve so that the feature will not run dry. An exact measurement of flow rate won't be known until you chat to the retailer. Just know what you want your pump to do, and let the retailer work everything out.

hard**sums**

One of the questions a retailer will ask when you are buying a pump is the volume of your water feature. This helps in selecting the correct pump for your pond. Most pump specifications are in litres, so it is sensible to use litres to calculate the volume of your water feature.

- Measure the length, depth and width of your water feature in metres.
- Multiply the length by the depth.
- Multiply that figure by the width.
- Finally, multiply the total by 1,000 to calculate the capacity of your water feature in litres. Easy.

That's fine for straight-edged ponds, but what about circular water features like the ones in Gardens 1 and 5?

- Measure the distance from the edge to the middle of your water feature.
- Multiply that figure by itself.
- Multiply that figure by 3.14.
- Multiply that figure by the depth of the feature.
- Finally, multiply that figure by 1,000 to calculate the capacity of your water feature in litres. Even easier.

- Above all, know what you want from your water feature.

In return you should ask a few questions to make sure the money you are parting with – and prices can vary enormously – is being wisely spent.

- Will the pump be running at full capacity, and will you have to change it if you upgrade your water feature at a later date?
- Does the pump have two outlets enabling two features to be run at the same time?
- Is it easy to disassemble, clean and reassemble? Have a go at this in the warmth of the retailer's showroom before having to try it on a winter's day.
- Is it easy to adjust the flow of water when you want to change the effects of your feature, or will you have to plunge your hands into freezing water to fiddle with dials?
- Can the pump be adjusted by remote control?
- Will the pump be ruined if your water feature runs dry for any reason, or does it have a cut-off fuse that can be reset?
- Is the pump guaranteed and, if so, for what?

plan**before**you**dig**

It is the easiest thing in the world to be swept along by the tide of water-feature enthusiasm, some say mania, and start digging just to get the water flowing. However, once a feature has been constructed it is difficult and time-consuming to change it. It's far better to get it right from the start.

Position your water feature in a place that is sheltered from strong winds and in a sunny part of the garden. If possible, avoid overhanging trees as their leaves will fall into the water and could clog up pumps and filters. In addition, their roots could damage inferior lining materials, and have even been known to crack concrete.

Electricity is generally required if a pump is going to be used. Decide where the cables and sockets will be situated before ploughing ahead. It is, for example, frustrating to rip up newly laid decking in order to bury the cable to the pump if all that was needed was a little thought at the planning stage.

The water feature in Garden 4 created visual interest and a seating area on an otherwise barren wall. Return pipes are hidden by terracotta drainage tiles and look superb.

water**safety**

Water and electricity are potentially a lethal combination. If you are at all unsure about installing electricity in the garden pay a qualified electrician to do the work.

Pumps are usually fitted with 10m (30ft) of cable. Manufacturers also supply extension leads and the correct connectors if required. The cable has to be buried in the soil but this produces, at a later stage, the danger of someone accidentally slicing through it with a spade. Feed it through a conduit for protection. This can be purchased ready-made, or you can improvise with reinforced hosepipe. Alternatively, use armoured cable to connect your pump to the mains source. Both methods of protection also stop the cable being degraded by water and stones in the soil.

Bury the cable at least 45cm (18in) deep and place a layer of flat roof-tiles over the top. Future gardeners digging in the area will suspect that electricity is close by when they see the tiles. Remember, if you move house someone else may be doing the digging.

The cable will be connected either to a three-pin plug and socket which involves drilling

In full flow the water pours over the tiled lip on its continuous journey. A stunning water feature.

through the house wall or to a weatherproof socket situated outdoors. Always use a residual current device (RCD) as a circuit-breaker. This plugs into normal three-pin sockets. The plug for the pump then slots into the device and the power is turned on. Nothing happens until a fault is detected, at which point the RCD shuts off the power source. This is done in a fraction of a second, before the electricity has a chance to harm whoever is touching the cable or pump – a simple, inexpensive way to save your life. It is possible to wire a complete house, and therefore every socket, to a specially manufactured RCD. This eliminates the need for a separate RCD on every socket. Contact a qualified electrician for details and installation. As an extra precaution, choose a low-voltage, 24-volt pump that works via a transformer situated in the house.

Choose your feature carefully, as all water attracts children and animals. You may not even know about visitors to your garden. Children may

do's&don'ts

✓ **do** plan a water feature carefully.

✗ **don't** build a water feature if young children use the garden.

✓ **do** place a water feature in a sunny site.

✗ **don't** place a water feature such as a fountain in a windy position as spray will drift, emptying the reservoir.

✓ **do** use a butyl liner if your budget allows.

✗ **don't** buy a pump just because it is cheap.

✓ **do** arm yourself with all the information required to choose the correct pump for your needs before visiting a retailer.

✗ **don't** place a pump directly on the floor of the water feature.

✓ **do** connect all electrical items to an RCD.

✗ **don't** try to install electrical items yourself if you lack the necessary expertise.

✓ **do** take time to enjoy your water feature.

wander into it when you aren't there, and animals may call at night. Be aware of the dangers and cover deep water with strong metal grid mesh.

waterfeatures**for**everyone

Water features figured prominently in the *Gardening Neighbours* designs, and all became distinctive elements of the gardens.

formal**fountains**

A formal round fountain is the focal point of Garden 1 with a powerful pump being used to jettison water metres into the air. Soil was excavated to allow the top of the water feature to be level with the surrounding borders and decking. The circular brickwork base was then constructed and lined with butyl. Once the butyl had moulded to the shape of the base, the overlap of liner at the top of the wall was disguised with brick edging. The top of the brick wall acts as a delightful seating area from which to admire the garden and water fountain.

Levelling is crucial in this kind of feature as water would otherwise slosh to one side. And a pump on an uneven base would send water in an unplanned direction, although it would be good for cleaning the house windows. The high

natural water-table in the garden, combined with heavy clay soil, resulted in puddles appearing around the feature. This was overcome by creating a soakaway and installing a pump near the base of the fountain to direct water to an area away from foot traffic.

An ingenious extra is that the flow of water can be controlled at a push of a button. The remote control changes the height of the fountain, the resultant sound of splashing water, the integral lighting and therefore the whole mood of the garden.

streams

A stream can look informal and wild in a garden setting. The stream in Garden 2 meanders across the width of the garden, creating opportunities for planting, the need for a bridge and the chance to use rocks and pebbles for a controlled yet natural appearance. In Garden 2, the stream 'was the pivotal feature on which the garden design was hung,' says Ali Ward. 'It was not an easy project but when you see the finished effect it is definitely worth it.' A stream requires a starting point, a route, a reservoir and a pump. If its total length is over 10m (30ft), a submersible pump will not be powerful enough and a surface one will be needed.

'Creating a natural looking feature like this one is much harder than a formal scheme'
Ali Ward, referring to the stream feature

The first stage of construction is to locate and dig the reservoir. This needs to be at the lowest point of the stream and will either house the submersible pump or be located close to the surface one.

If your garden is near level, just dig out the soil in the shape of the stream and along

Woven membrane placed on top of the liner ensures that stones that will form the stream bed in Garden 2 do not tear the lining.

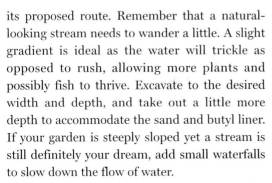

Once liner and woven membrane are in place, pebbles or gravel that form the stream bed in Garden 4 are put in place.

its proposed route. Remember that a natural-looking stream needs to wander a little. A slight gradient is ideal as the water will trickle as opposed to rush, allowing more plants and possibly fish to thrive. Excavate to the desired width and depth, and take out a little more depth to accommodate the sand and butyl liner. If your garden is steeply sloped yet a stream is still definitely your dream, add small waterfalls to slow down the flow of water.

Once the course of the stream has been dug line the base either with a 5cm (2in) layer of sand or with non-woven liner. This protects the butyl, which goes on next, from damage. The edges of the butyl will form an overlap into the side borders where they can be weighed down and hidden by pebbles, slabs or any other covering. On gentle slopes, carefully place pebbles on the butyl liner along the length of the stream. For steep gradients, put a layer of cement 5cm (2in) on the liner and stick stones into the mix. Connect the pipe that will return water from the reservoir to the head of the stream and bury it in the soil.

Fill the reservoir with water, put a submersible pump in it or connect the surface pump and switch on. After a few agonizing gurgles and splutters, water will soon begin to move along the stream. Check the level of water every day for a week, and ensure that the reservoir is covered by a secure grid and pebbles.

wall-**mounted**water**features**

Wall-mounted features are popular but do present a problem. For water to cascade from an outlet, fall a metre or so into a limpid pool and circulate back to the outlet, you need pipes. The pipes take water back up from the pool or, in the case the feature in Garden 4, from a reservoir

several metres away after a journey down a pebbled stream and around a magnificent circle of wooden decking.

There are three ways to tackle this problem. One is to drill a hole in the wall and run return pipes through, and then up, the back of the wall. This could involve obtaining permission from your neighbour or, if the feature is attached to the house wall, pipes running inside the home.

Another, more creative, option is to disguise the pipes that run up the wall to the start of the feature. In Garden 4 they were fixed to the wall and covered with square terracotta drainage pipes. Spare roof-tiles from the house can also be used to create a harmonious design.

The third option is to use decorative pipes that look great from the word go.

The feature in Garden 4 has a few added extras. The water falls from the outlet pipe into a raised pool, the edge of which is at ideal sitting height, and flows over a lip. It then begins a circuitous route along a pebble-lined stream and around a decking platform before disappearing into a reservoir and eventually being pumped back to the start.

The basic water-feature principles were used in all the *Gardening Neighbour* gardens with sand, a non-woven liner and finally butyl liner underpinning fantastic designs.

statue**features**

Water features made from statues are classics, and provide focal points in large areas like the lawn in Garden 8. The design is simple, comprising a large, butyl-lined reservoir containing a pump, a grid covered with pebbles and a pipe that carries water from the reservoir up through the base of a decorative statue to an appropriate outlet. An alternative to butyl liner is the kind of rigid plastic tank used in home hot or cold water systems.

In statue features the water falls elegantly from the outlet, down the statue, through the pebbles on the grid, into the reservoir and is circulated through the statue. They look great, sound relaxing and are easy to construct. The hardest part is deciding on the style of statue. Alternatives to a Roman god or goddess are a Cretan urn, a large terracotta pot, a boulder with holes drilled in it – or indeed anything you fancy. Ensure that the grid and surroundings are firm enough to carry the weight of a statue or ornament, and secure any object that may move to a base.

Water trickles back on to the pebbles, down into the reservoir, and is then pumped back through the statue in Garden 8.

water-featurekits

A complete kit is a good way to get started with a water feature. The kits comprise a round reservoir, a pump with interchangeable nozzles and a slatted plastic lid. Interchangeable nozzles allow changes to the effects the water feature produces. Installation involves excavating a hole, placing the kit in it, firming around the kit with sieved soil, filling the reservoir with water, plugging in the pump and standing back. This is, after all, what all water features are, give or take a few minor details.

decorations

Fountain heads: Attachments for fountain heads produce a number of different effects. A spouting geyser is popular, with bubbling, foamy water *de rigueur* in the features in Gardens 1 and 5. Fountains can be delicate, they can pirouette, they can form bell shapes and can even be set to music. When purchasing a pump, check that different attachments are included or are readily available. Experiment to find out the best effects for your particular garden.

Scented water: Designers have created features where the water is scented. Perhaps not economical for long-term use, but fantastic for an evening get-together with friends. Do check that scented oils, such as lavender, are safe for fish and plants.

Coloured water: Water can be coloured to add extra interest, especially where a design calls for near-transparent sheets of water to fall over surfaces. Colours are available from aquatic centres but, once again, check the safety aspects.

Edgings: Edging a water feature is essential and an opportunity to be creative. Bricks, as used in many of the gardens, give a solid look to a design and the edgings also provide seating where you can stop, relax and admire the feature. When constructing such an edging, take care not to leave cement on the bricks as it is devilishly difficult to remove, resulting in unsightly staining, and its dust is highly toxic to plants and animals. Set bricks or slabs with a slight overhang. This looks great and protects the lining from exposure to the sun.

Pebbles, rocks and boulders: Pebbles help to create a natural look and provide a graduated edge to streams. Use a mix of different sizes, rather than one standard size, for a more natural look. Rocks and boulders are used extensively in the *Gardening Neighbours* gardens. In the stream in Garden 2 they create natural barriers to the water flow and the way the water moves as a result creates colour changes on the pebbles below the surface. They also provide shady areas for fish and anchorage points for plants. Choosing rocks and boulders is tricky, as ideally they should be of local origin to complement your surroundings. Always get large ones delivered to your garden, as close as possible to where you want to position them. Use a crowbar or wheeled truck to move heavy items.

Bridges: You need to step carefully over even the narrowest of streams to avoid scuffing pebbles into the water or damaging liners so it's necessary to have bridges in areas of busy foot traffic. The one leading to the summer house in Garden 2 is an excellent example. Bridges must be sympathetic to the overall garden design. Ones made from rustic poles look terrific in a wildlife or country garden, but the stone slab in Garden 2 is in keeping with the colours and textures of the stream.

(top) Slate chippings lead to a tile lip in Garden 3.

(middle) Different sized pebbles form the beach area in Garden 4's water feature.

(bottom) The Garden 2 bridge allows easy access to the other river bank.

Slate chippings and shards: These were used in Garden 3 with spectacular results. The canal winding through the wavy lawn was constructed in the usual way using sand, non-woven liner and finally butyl liner. Tons of blue slate was gently poured on top of this to a depth of 10cm (4in). The water seeps between the chippings and shards, and instead of forming a fast-flowing stream creates a floating, suspended animation, moving imperceptibly down the slight gradient to the waiting reservoir. The slate surface varies between being wet and dry, and the sun plays on the colours inherent in the chippings. A magical look to a fantastic water feature.

green**without**envy

A newly created water feature or pond can look murky. It's not a problem with fast-flowing streams, but the dreaded algae can strike at any time. These microscopic plants proliferate in strong sunlight and when there is an excess of nutrients in the water. The fresh tap water used to fill water features is often high in nutrients

and gardeners can therefore initially expect strong growth of algae. As a pond gains an ecological balance, as nutrients are used up and not replaced, as plants grow, the water will clear.

Algae can return if this balance is upset, for example by nutrients leaching into the water from lawn or flower fertilizers. Take care when

leaky**water**features

Don't automatically assume you have a leak just because the level of water in your feature drops. In hot weather evaporation can account for 2.5cm (1in) water loss a week in both large and small water features.

- Check that water isn't being blown out of the reservoir catchment area by high winds. If it is, and with fountains this is a common problem, alter the spray setting to compensate for wind loss. With a new water feature check that the liner isn't kinked and allowing water to flow over the sides.

- If none of these problems apply, turn off the pump and observe the water level over a couple of days. If it drops slowly you only have a small leak or crack to deal with. A fast drop accompanied by a soaking patch close to the feature indicates a bigger problem.

- Leave the pump off and wait for the water level to stabilize, then inspect the lining at the new level closely. There will probably be a crack or split somewhere. Once located, use a pond repair kit, similar to one for mending bicycle punctures, for a hole in a butyl liner. Kits for rigid-pool liners are also available.

- If you can't locate the problem, check all connections and seals to the pump. Also check the reservoir, often a troublemaker in a new water feature, for cracks. Check everything you can before emptying the feature of water, pebbles, boulders, slate chippings and plants. If you see a crack or tear, get going with the repair kit.

- If you still can't spot the problem the only solution is to lay a new liner over the old one and start refilling. Do remember that even the smallest of stones can cause rips in butyl, especially when you are cleaning a feature out. Take care to avoid costly, time-consuming mistakes.

applying these. Overfeeding fish can cause algae to grow for the same reason. Dead leaves, plants and fish left to rot in the water will also create an imbalance of nutrients, as will introducing plants that are growing in nutrient-rich compost. Always use specially manufactured aquatic compost, with low levels of nutrients, for all water features. Regularly clearing up leaves and other debris will reduce algae growth.

Patience is necessary when waiting for a pond or water feature to clear. It takes at least three growing seasons for all the components to get to know each other and settle into a clear routine. Of course, patience is a virtue, but not one that every gardener has, or even needs: buying and fitting a filter containing an ultraviolet light bulb will sort out problem algae within days. The water passes through the filter and the light causes the algae to clump together, forming larger, heavier colonies that sink to the bottom of the pond. There are also chemical treatments for algae, but it is better to get a feature ecologically balanced before resorting to drastic measures. Natural treatments and biological filters encourage an increase in bacterial activity, which reduces the algae, and are therefore environmentally safer.

The other scourge of water features is blanket weed. It can choke a still-water feature within days and, again, is the result of an imbalance of nutrients. It's not such a problem in moving water, where the bubbling oxygen reduces most algae problems. Chemical treatments are available, but they kill the weed which in turn rots, releasing nutrients back into the water and encouraging more algae to grow. Physically removing blanket weed is the safest option. As it's a bigger alga it can be scooped out and put on the compost heap. Allow time — about a day — for tadpoles and other creatures to escape and return to the water before moving scooped-out blanketweed from the side of the pond to the compost heap.

Duckweed is a spiteful little plant that covers the surface of ponds and still-water features with a thick, green overcoat. It cuts out light and kills off plant and animal life. As it is often introduced by purchasing contaminated plants it is good practice to wash the roots of all imports before allowing them into a feature. Duckweed doesn't like water that's on the move, so consider installing a fountain to create an effervescent, youthful-looking water feature with a clear complexion.

plants**for**water**features**

Plants are capable of growing in the desert, in tropical rainforests and in freezing conditions. Some even relish the prospect of having their roots and stems covered in water all year round. These aquatic plants are a specialized group, and can be divided into three main cliques.

oxygenating**plants**

Oxygenating plants are essential as they absorb carbon dioxide and nutrients from the water, helping maintain its often fragile balance. Roots, stems and leaves are submerged but flowers can sometimes be seen above the surface. All types need a sunny position. Buy oxygenators in bunches from an aquatic-plant retailer, plant them in baskets in a mix of sand and gravel and place them on the bottom of the pond.

Goldfish weed (botanically known as *Lagarosiphon major*, but still labelled *Elodea crispa*), is the most common oxygenator. It has brittle stems and narrow, curly leaves that form a dense, slithery mass of vegetation. It can spread forever, so must be thinned out every year.

Water buttercup (*Ranunculus aquatilis*) has clover-like leaves, both submerged and floating, and white flowers in summer. Another plant that will spread once established, so keep a close eye on this individual.

deep-water**plants**

Deep-water plants look fantastic and provide shade, which is vital in keeping down algae populations. They are easily planted by carefully lowering baskets contining the plants into the centres of ponds.

Water lilies (*Nymphaea*) are beautiful and serene, but don't like being splashed with water so are ruled out of vigorous fountains. There is a wide range available, with flowers of varying sizes and colours.

Nymphaea tetragona produces star-shaped white flowers 3cm (1¼in) in diameter throughout summer. It spreads to 30cm (12in) and has dark green leaves.

N. 'James Brydon' is a popular mid-sized water lily that produces fragrant, orange-red flowers 15cm (6in) in diameter throughout summer. The plants spread to 2.5m (8ft). Be careful when checking out the fragrance of plants in the middle of a large water feature.

N. 'Gladstoneana' is a big beauty with star-shaped white flowers 30cm (12in) in diameter on plants that spread to 3m (12ft).

Flower colour varies enormously between different varieties of water lilies, with plenty of white blooms available. *N.* 'Amabilis' produces pink flowers, *N.* 'Blue Beauty' a gorgeous deep blue bloom, *N.* 'Red Flare' a fiery red flower and *N.* 'Odorata Sulphurea Grandiflora' a spectacular yellow. Whichever variety you choose, remove leaves that fade to prevent them rotting in the water.

Golden club (*Orontium aquaticum*) is an intriguing plant that produces gold and white flower spikes in spring. They emerge from the blue-green floating leaves and last for weeks. The plant spreads 60cm (2ft) in still water.

marginal**plants**

The roots of marginal plants are submerged but the stems and leaves are above the surface of the water. They do not contribute to its balance, but they look terrific, soften hard edges and provide shelter for wildlife. Plant them into hessian-lined pond baskets filled with aquatic compost. Never be tempted to use garden compost as it contains too many nutrients. Place the baskets on shelves in ponds or in the boggy pebble area around streams.

Beardless Japanese iris (*Iris laevigata*) produces blue, blue-white or pure white flowers in early summer. The plant grows to 90cm (3ft) and spreads as far as you allow it to – probably around the perimeter of a water feature. Grows vigorously in full sun or semi-shade, but must have its roots in mud or water. Plant *I. laevigata* 'Variegata' for its interesting leaf colour: green and cream stripes. It is capable of flowering a second time in mid-autumn.

Typha latifolia has clumps of green leaves that are perfect for surrounding a water feature and creating shelter for animals. Grows well in shade or sun, and must have its roots in water. Beige flowers are followed by the dark brown seed heads in late summer. It should only be considered for a large pond or water feature as it grows to 2.5m (8ft) and is invasive. A pocket-sized version for smaller water features is dwarf reedmace (*T. minima*). It grows to 60cm (2ft), doesn't spread beyond 2.5m (8ft) and still produces brown heads on thin leaves. It's great for any water feature that requires the natural look.

Bog bean, buckbean (*Menyanthes trifoliata*) is a lovely marginal plant with mid-green leaves divided into three parts. Spring flowers are white and fringed at the edges. A controlled plant by aquatic standards, it grows to 25cm (10in) high with a spread of 30cm (12in). Prefers a sunny position on the margins of a feature.

Yellow skunk cabbage (*Lysichiton americanus*) is a vigorous marginal plant that grows 1m (3ft) high with a similar spread. Yellow blooms push their way up through the mud before fleshy green leaves appear in spring. Prefers a sunny position but will tolerate shade. Ideal for the margins of both still- and sparkling-water features.

Houttuynia cordata 'Chameleon' is an invasive marginal plant that will grow anywhere you provide moisture for its roots. Green leaves are splashed with red and yellow and are produced in early spring. Small white flowers appear in

Typha minima

summer. A sunny position at the edge of a feature will bring out the best coloration, but plants will grow in the shade. Grows 10cm (4in) high and will spread forever.

fishponds

Fish are a delightful addition to a pond but it must be large enough to cater for their needs. A minimum depth of 1m (3ft) is needed to prevent it freezing solid in winter. This depth of water also stays cool in summer. Oxygenating plants are essential to keep the water clear, oxygenated and the fish healthy. There should be plenty of shelter from predators and the sun. Much of this can be provided by plants in and around the pond.

It is also vital not to overstock a pond because the fish will become stressed and possibly die. As a guideline 15cm (6in) of fish, be it one large fish or several smaller ones, requires 45cm (18in) of water. When calculating how many fish you can have, bear in mind that they will grow and build this into your calculations. Smaller fish settle into their new surroundings much more easily than their bigger brothers and sisters. Always buy from a reputable dealer and choose lively fish with bright eyes and no chunks missing from their fins.

Take your time introducing fish to a new pond. Wait up to three months for plants to settle down, leaks and creaks to be ironed out and the ecosystem to begin to balance before contemplating adding them. Fish are best introduced in late spring when the water has warmed up naturally and the chance of penetrating frosts has diminished.

To allow them to acclimatize to the water and its temperature leave them in their bags on the surface of the pond for about twenty or thirty minutes. Then open the bag and allow the fish to swim out when they are ready – don't tip them into the pond.

There are two schools of thought when it comes to feeding fish. The first is to leave them to fend for themselves and learn to eat mosquito larvae and generally become self-sufficient – all perfectly possible in a well-balanced pond stocked with plants and wildlife. The second is to feed your fish which will encourage them to come

Place fish food in a floating plastic hoop to prevent it disappearing along a fast-flowing stream, such as in Garden 2.

to the surface allowing you to admire their colour and markings. If you do feed your fish, make sure excess food is removed from the surface of the pond. In the running stream in Garden 2 flakes are placed in a plastic hoop which stops them dispersing along the whole length of the stream, and also prevents flakes entering the reservoir where it would prove awkward to remove them. It is also easier for the fish to feed, as chasing after fast-moving flakes must be exhausting.

which**fish**?

The choice of fish for outdoor cold-water ponds is terrific, and choosing favourites can provide hours of family fun.

Koi carp are the first fish that spring to many gardeners' minds, but they require a large pond at least 1.5m (6ft) deep. They are also expensive and produce more waste than other fish – a filtration system is recommended if large quantities are planned for your pond. However, they are beautiful and worth the effort required to keep them looking pristine and healthy. Specially formulated feed for koi carp, designed to bring out their colour, is available from aquatic-fish retailers.

Common goldfish are colourful, readily available and fun for children. Because of their bright colour and habit of feeding near the top of a pond, they are easily seen, unlike darker green or brown fish which can melt into the background. They are brilliant as starter fish in a small pond, but do ensure that the water doesn't freeze over in winter. Installing a pond heater will keep a hole in the ice.

Comet goldfish are the same colour but have gracefully long fins and flowing tails. They are perfect for small ponds.

Shubunkins are extravagantly coloured with black, red, orange and yellow blotches on a near-transparent body. They are another good fish for the smaller pond as they grow to a maximum of 20cm (8cm).

Sarasa comets are slightly larger, growing to a maximum length of 30cm (12in), and have orange markings on a white body that sports elegant fins and a flowing tail. They need a larger pond.

Golden orfe and golden rudd, both gloriously golden-coloured fish, need bigger ponds that give them space to feed and develop.

maintaining**a**water**feature**

SPRING

- If possible drain the feature and then clean it, check for cracks, rips or holes, repair these and refill.
- Divide and thin out exuberant plants such as water lilies.
- Push aquatic-plant food into baskets containing plants that are a couple of years old. Never sprinkle plant food of any type over the surface of a water feature. Doing so will only encourage algae.
- Plant new aquatic plants in the sediment at the bottom of ponds or in planting baskets lined with hessian and filled with aquatic compost.
- Remove, clean and carefully store any pond heaters employed over the winter. Begin to feed active fish.

SUMMER

- Check and top up water levels as the features will be in constant use and hot days cause water to evaporate. Do this regularly as a severe drop in water level may expose liners to the sun, or even damage expensive pumps. Plants require a constant level to maintain healthy growth.
- Remove dead flower heads to prevent unwanted seedlings appearing in the pond, causing congestion.
- Continue to plant aquatic plants.
- Clean the pump regularly to prevent blockages.
- Continue to feed fish. Remove unwanted food 30 minutes after they have stopped feeding.

AUTUMN

- Clear fallen leaves from the surface of all water features.
- If possible, stretch fine mesh netting over a pond or open reservoir to stop leaves falling into the water. This can be removed when all the trees in the near vicinity are bare.
- Cut all dead leaves and flowers off plants.
- Continue to feed active fish.

WINTER

- Prevent your pond freezing over by installing a specially designed heater, or, if you do not have fish in your water feature, drain all the water and refill in spring.
- In severe weather switch off the pump, remove it from the water feature and take it indoors to clean it.
- Cover small water features with sacking to prevent plants or pump being damaged.
- Fish will now be dormant so stop feeding them.

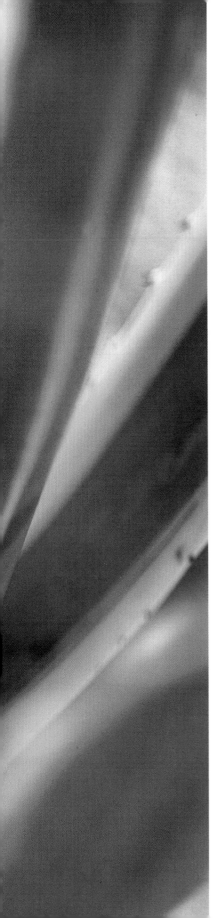

chapterfour

plants

plant *n.* any living organism that typically synthesizes its food from inorganic substances, lacks specialized sense organs, and has no power of locomotion.

adictionary definition cannot convey the full meaning of plants. Words will never express the feeling as your heart skips a beat at the sight of a woodland floor awash with bluebells. A gardener cannot explain the flush of excitement at discovering a tray of vulnerable seedlings blinking in the dawn sun, or the flood of emotion when planting a tree to celebrate the arrival of a new member of the family. The same family who may gather around a table and enjoy the fruits, and vegetables, of their labours. Plants evoke memories of the past, consume thoughts and actions in the present and represent the future. They also look great.

Each of the *Gardening Neighbours* gardens contains beautiful plants. Some are crammed with vegetation, shrubs rubbing shoulders with trees which in turn provide gentle shade from the hot sun. Chris and Ali have got their plants working hard, none more so than in the borders in Garden 5, designed with medicine in mind. Here all the plants have some element of yellow, fantastic textural changes and each of the beauties has hidden powers.

Even in the garden with the fewest plants, Garden 4, their charm and elegance are shown off to perfection. Each and every garden has a combination of plants that will thrive together, forming distinctive and beautiful lasting designs. They allow a garden to evolve, to change not only from year to year but through each of the seasons.

Each of the gardens will look terrific all the year round, thanks to fantastic design and great plant selection. Pick and mix from the following line-up to create a stunning garden twelve months of the year.

springinterest

Spring is a shiny, sparkly season in the garden. Buds swell, leaves unfurl, with anticipation and expectancy reaching fever pitch.

Drumstick primrose (*Primula denticulata*)
Rounded heads of purple or pink blooms crown stout flower spikes that arise from a dense rosette of green leaves. Plants naturally produce clumps to cover the ground.
Height: 50cm (20in).
Spread: 50cm (20in).
Soil: any moist soil, rich in organic matter.
Light level: partial shade.
One season wonder?: a wonderful spring plant but leaves look average the rest of the year.
National or local?: fully hardy throughout the UK.
Aftercare: take precautions against slugs and snails.

Bugle (*Ajuga reptans* 'Atropurpurea')
A free-spreading evergreen with dark purple leaves, perfect as a striking ground-cover plant. Short flowers spikes support blue flowers. Looks fantastic growing in colour-contrasting pebbles and gravel.
Height: 15cm (6in).
Spread: 90cm (3ft).
Soil: any soil; displays exuberant growth in moist conditions.
Light levels: sun or shade.
One season wonder?: foliage looks stunning all year with flowers in spring and sometimes autumn.
Local or national?: a tough customer, fully hardy throughout the UK.
Aftercare: increase stock by lifting and dividing clumps in spring, and replanting.

Division Large clumps of perennials can be lifted in autumn or early spring using a garden fork. Tease or even rip apart smaller plants, each containing a small section of root, and replant in a new position. These new plants will quickly establish and form large plants.

Drumstick primrose

plant**choice**

Chris's choice 'It's almost impossible to choose a favourite, but one that is guaranteed to bring a smile to a gardener's face when they hear the name is *Metasequoia glyptostroboides*. It's an excellent tree with an extraordinary history and it works so hard at providing year round interest'.

Ali's choice '*Buxus sempervirens* is one of my favourite plants. It might be perceived as being slightly ordinary in many ways, but it is a good solid green block suitable for hedging, sculpting into topiary or letting grow loose into a large bush.'

Chris's container choice '*Geranium palmatum* – it produces cerise pink flowers from spring to the first frosts, has great glossy heavily divided leaves and provides a slash of red in the frosts. Ideal for any patio or terrace.'

Lady's mantle (*Alchemilla mollis*)
Lime-green leaves appear in early spring. They are covered with fine hairs that trap moisture droplets and turn their surfaces into glittering displays in the morning sun.
Height: 50cm (20in).
Spread: 50cm (20in).
Soil: prefers dry soil; tolerates moist conditions, but avoid waterlogging at all costs.
Light level: sun or shade.
One season wonder?: wonderful spring growth; fluffy yellow flowers appear in summer.
Local or national?: successful around the UK.
Aftercare: cut the plants down to ground level in late summer to encourage more of that fresh, zesty growth.

Coral flower (*Heuchera micrantha* var. *diversifolia* 'Palace Purple')

The deep purple leaves are ever-present throughout the year, but it's the high gloss of new foliage that makes this an outstanding spring plant.

Height: 45cm (18in).

Spread: 45cm (18in).

Soil: any moist, well-drained soil.

Light level: shade for part of the day; never in baking sun.

One season wonder?: leaves are the mainstay of the plant's attraction, with white flowers on wiry stems a summer bonus.

Local or national?: protect from severe, prolonged frost by covering the crowns of plants with straw.

Aftercare: cut leaves and use them in flower arrangements; this will encourage even more growth.

Pittosporum tenuifolium

The skeleton of black stems is clothed with wavy-edged, green leaves throughout the year. Purple, honey-scented flowers are produced on strong-growing plants in spring.

Height: 6m (20ft).

Spread: 6m (20ft).

Soil: well-drained, neutral or slightly acidic sandy soil.

Light level: sun or shade for part of the day.

One season wonder?: essential evergreen backbone to a year-round garden.

Local or national?: requires a warm, sheltered spot, similar to the south-facing gardens in *Gardening Neighbours.*

Aftercare: grow against a warm wall to ensure success.

Ostrich fern (*Matteuccia struthiopteris*)

A magnificent fern. Light green outer fronds hug dark green inner ones to produce a living shuttlecock. An impressive, eye-catching plant.

Height: 1m (3ft).

more**spring**sensations

Chocolate vine (*Akebia quinata*) vanilla-scented, purple flowers on a lovely climbing plant.

Golden hop (*Humulus lupulus* 'Aureus') a stunning climbing plant with yellow leaves.

Exochorda x _macrantha_ 'The Bride' billowing white flowers on a medium-sized shrub.

Broom (*Cytisus* x *praecox* 'Warminster') medium-sized shrub smothered in pea-like, butter-yellow flowers.

Flame of the forest (*Pieris* 'Forest Flame') fiery new growth and white flowers on a large shrub.

Pittosporum tenuifolium

Spread: 45cm (18in).

Soil: wet all the time and rich in organic matter.

Light level: shade for part of the day.

One season wonder?: fantastic to see croziers unfurl in spring; summer fronds provide a strong backdrop for other plants, but nothing interesting in autumn or winter.

Local or national?: fully hardy throughout the UK.

Aftercare: remove faded fronds to maintain the beauty of the plants.

summerinterest

Plants are in overdrive and effortlessly produce magnificent floral displays for weeks on end. Colour and perfume are everywhere on boisterous plants in borders and containers.

Penstemon 'Garnet'

Deep wine-red flowers are produced on spikes above fresh apple-green leaves. Blooms appear in midsummer and add vibrancy to colour schemes.

Height: 60cm (2ft).
Spread: 60cm (2ft).
Soil: any well-drained, sandy soil.
Light level: full sun.
One season wonder?: long flowering period from midsummer to autumn; no interest in winter.
Local or national?: wet winters can damage plants.
Aftercare: leave old stems *in situ* over the winter as these protect plants; prune in early spring to encourage vigorous growth.

Penstemon

African lily

(*Agapanthus* 'Headbourne Hybrids')
Flower clusters, coloured a sensational blue, crown tall stalks.

Height: 60cm (2ft).
Spread: 60cm (2ft).
Soil: any dry soil.
Light level: full sun.
One season wonder?: leaves remain well into winter; nothing of interest until spring growth and summer flowers.
Local or national?: no problems in warm areas; take care in cold spots.
Aftercare: place containers on their sides to prevent winter rain rotting the plants.

Nemesia denticulata

Produce masses of flowers in a wide colour range and are easy to grow. This is *the* summer flower for containers and borders.

Height: 30cm (12in).
Spread: 15cm (6in).
Soil: any moist soil.
Light level: full sun.
One season wonder?: flowers all summer; nothing of interest in autumn and winter.
Local or national?: grows throughout the UK.
Aftercare: keep well watered; take cuttings off your best plants in autumn for next year's stock.

Delphinium grandiflorum 'Blue Butterfly'

This plant's blooms are an intense deep blue and are produced on flower spikes around midsummer.

Height: 45cm (18in).
Spread: 30cm (12in).
Soil: any well-drained soil, rich in organic matter.
Light level: full sun.

Cuttings Using a clean gardening knife or sharp secateurs, remove 10 cm (4 in) of stem, to include the growing tip. Remove lower leaves and plant in pots of well-drained compost. Do not allow to dry out. Keep out of scorching sun and roots will form shortly.

African lily   *Nemesia denticulata*

Delphinium grandiflorum

Ophiopogon planiscapus

One season wonder?: blooms in summer, sometimes into autumn and dies down in winter; spring growth looks so fresh that slugs and snails can't resist it.

Local or national?: hardy throughout the UK.

Aftercare: encourage a second flush of blooms by removing faded flower spikes.

Gaura lindheimeri

A graceful plant with white, tubular blooms often flashed with delicate pink. Flower spikes are produced in July and last until the first frosts.

Height: 1m (3ft).

Spread: 1m (3ft).

Soil: sandy, slightly acidic, well-drained and dry.

Light level: full sun.

One season wonder?: flowers persevere until early autumn, but no interest in winter.

Local or national?: given the correct conditions, hardy throughout the UK.

Aftercare: watch for self-sown seedlings and replant these where you want them.

Blanket flower

Plants that cannot withstand the cold or wet in winter are lifted, placed in pots and stored in cool, frost-free conditions.

Ophiopogon planiscapus 'Nigrescens'

Clumps of black, grass-like leaves create a stunning plant. Lilac flowers are produced in July, followed by black berries in autumn.

Height: 15cm (6in).

Spread: 30cm (12in).

Soil: any soil that is rich in organic matter and well drained.

Light level: full sun.

One season wonder?: leaves are present all the year round; flowers in summer; berries in autumn and winter.

Local or national?: wherever you are in the UK either cover or lift plants in extremely cold weather.

Aftercare: carefully lift large plants in spring and tease apart young plantlets for replanting.

Blanket flower

(*Gaillardia* x *grandiflora* varieties)

Bold flowers in shades of orange, yellow and red. Daisy-like blooms crown plants from summer through to autumn.

Height: 90cm (3ft).

Spread: 50cm (20in).

Soil: must be well-drained; acid or alkaline.

Light level: full sun; ideal for the south-facing *Gardening Neighbours* gardens.

One season wonder?: long flowering period but no winter or spring action.

Local or national?: fully hardy throughout the UK.

Aftercare: lift, divide and replant clumps of plants every three years to prevent straggly growth.

Potato vine (*Solanum laxum* 'Album')

A scrambling, clambering climber that produces clusters of gorgeous, pure white flowers in late summer amid dark green leaves.

Potato vine

Height: 6m (20ft).

Spread: 6m (20ft).

Soil: any soil but must be well drained.

Light level: full sun.

One season wonder?: long flowering period, sometimes lasting into autumn; loses some leaves in cold winters; no spring interest.

Local or national?: borderline hardy and often damaged by severe frosts.

Aftercare: grow against a warm wall or in a frost-free site.

Cranesbill (*Geranium* species)

One of the easiest plants to grow, with masses of blooms in shades of blue, pink and white. Fantastic at supressing weed growth. Try G. 'Johnson's Blue'.

Height: 30cm (12in).

Spread: 60cm (2ft).

Soil: any well-drained soil rich in organic matter.

Light level: full sun; some varieties may need shade.

One season wonder?: deep lavender-blue flowers throughout summer; attractive leaves throughout the year.

Local or national?: tough, hardy throughout the UK.

Aftercare: self-sown seedlings appear in every nook and cranny. Weed out unwanted ones and replant them.

Cranesbill

Montbretia (*Crocosmia* species)

Major player in the yellow planting scheme in Garden 5. Many species also produce arching flower spikes of orange or red blooms.

Height: 90cm (3ft).

Spread: 20cm (8in).

Soil: well-drained sandy soil.

Light level: sunny.

One season wonder?: sword-like leaves are impressive in spring; flowers in summer, occasionally persisting until autumn; no winter interest.

Local or national?: most species are hardy but check labels as some need to be lifted and stored over winter.

Aftercare: do not remove dead foliage in winter as this protects the crowns.

Agave americana 'Striata'

Blue-green leaves are banded with yellow and edged with vicious teeth. Flower spike of white

Agave americana

blooms erupts from the central rosette in this desert-look plant.

Height: 2m (6ft).

Spread: 2m (6ft).

Soil: well-drained, sandy soil.

Light level: full sun.

One season wonder?: leaves last all year round and blooms survive for weeks.

Local or national?: not for the great outdoors from September to April.

Aftercare: take indoors in early autumn to a cool, light position and reduce watering; take back out in spring.

Japanese aralia *(Fatsia japonica)*

Large, glossy leaves make this beauty a must for the tropical-look garden. Highly polished foliage lasts all year round, with coral-like autumn flowers a bonus.

Height: 3m (10ft).

Spread: 3m (10ft).

Soil: any well-drained soil rich in organic matter.

Light level: partial shade.

One season wonder?: evergreen, with flowers in autumn.

Local or national?: avoid planting in windy sites.

Aftercare: only prune if your plant gets too big; don't be alarmed if leaves droop after a frost as they always recover.

more**summer**sizzlers

Phygelius aequalis pale red flowers with yellow throats on a small shrub in midsummer.

Chilean glory vine (*Eccremocarpus scaber*) masses of orange-red blooms on a rampant climber.

Verbena bonariensis wiry stems of purple flowers above a medium-sized perennial.

Oriental poppy (*Papaver orientale* 'Allegro') outstanding paper-thin, red blooms on a medium-sized perennial.

Campanula poscharskyana a rampant spreading plant covered in violet blooms.

Japanese aralia

autumninterest

Far from being a time to wind down, many plants are in full flow or just beginning to shine in the misty, romance-filled days of autumn.

Buckthorn
(Rhamnus alaternus var. 'Argenteovariegata')
An impressive name for a powerful, evergreen plant with leathery, glossy, grey-green leaves; red berries in autumn and winter.
Height: 3m (10ft).
Spread: 3m (10ft).
Soil: any soil rich in organic matter.
Light level: sun or shade for part of the day.
One season wonder?: evergreen; berries in autumn and winter and fresh leaf growth in spring.
Local or national?: hardy everywhere in the UK if sheltered from cold winds.
Aftercare: ensure success by growing against a fence for shelter.

Cone flower *(Rudbeckia* species)
A fantastic addition to a border or container where bright yellow, orange or mahogany-red blooms are needed. Plants are easy to please and eager to reward.
Height: 1m (3ft).
Spread: 60cm (2ft).
Soil: any well-drained or moist soil.
Light level: sun or shade.
One season wonder?: lush leaf growth in spring and summer; flowers in autumn.
Local or national?: grows well everywhere in the UK.
Aftercare: support or stake to avoid plants flopping onto the soil and spoiling the blooms.

Golden rod *(Solidago* 'Golden Wings')
Feathery panicles of tiny yellow flowers grace plants in early autumn. A vigorous plant with mid-green leaves, it is an invaluable member of the year-round garden and Garden 5.
Height: 1.5m (5ft).

Buckthorn

Cone flower

Golden rod

Spread: 1m (3ft).

Soil: any well-drained soil.

Light level: sun or shade for part of the day.

One season wonder?: leave flower heads on the plants for winter birds and self-seeding.

Local or national?: a tough customer wherever it's grown.

Aftercare: prune out unwanted shoots to prevent the plant taking over your borders.

Japanese anemone
(*Anemone* x *hybrida* varieties)

Flower production reaches a crescendo in autumn. Punctuate your border plants with classically simple red, pink, purple or white blooms. Beware, as it can take over.

Height: 1.5m (5ft).

Spread: 60cm (2ft).

Soil: any well-drained soil.

Light level: full sun or partial shade.

One season wonder?: spring and summer foliage build up to a fantastic floral display in autumn.

Local or national?: just try stopping them.

Aftercare: plants will pop up everywhere so pull out unwanted specimens.

Hardy plumbago
(*Ceratostigma willmottianum*)

For flowers and autumn colour this cracker takes some beating. A combination of blue blooms and fiery red foliage makes it a delightful addition to the border.

Height: 1.5m (5ft).

Spread: 1.5m (5ft).

Soil: any well-drained soil.

Light level: sunny.

One season wonder?: new growth in spring;

Japanese anemone   Hardy plumbago

Pruning Cut branches that are diseased or impeding light. Growers of topiary specimens are often pruning every week. Sharp, clean secateurs or pruning saws should be used.

dense foliage in summer and a spectacular autumn show.

Local or national?: hard winters may kill some branches, but rarely entire plants.

Aftercare: prune back dead branches in spring to encourage strong growth.

Michaelmas daisies (*Aster* species)

Blue or purple daisy-like blooms are delightful in the soft sunshine of clear autumn afternoons. Lots of choice, all guaranteed to add colour to your garden. Try *A.* x *frikartii* 'Mönch'.

Height: 90cm (3ft).

Spread: 45cm (18in).

Soil: well-drained soil rich in organic matter.

Light level: sun or partial shade.

One season wonder?: flowers may appear in late summer; brilliant autumn blooms; not much winter or spring activity.

Local or national?: hardy throughout the UK.

Aftercare: to help prevent attacks by mildew make sure the plants never become short of water in summer.

Smoke bush

(*Cotinus coggygria* 'Golden Spirit')

Relative newcomer to the scene with sensational yellow foliage throughout the year and incredible changes in colour every autumn. A stunning plant.

Height: 5m (15ft).

Spread: 5m (15ft).

Soil: any soil rich in organic matter.

Light level: full sun.

One season wonder?: new growth appears in late spring; yellow foliage all summer; red and orange firecracker autumn changes.

Local or national?: hardy throughout the UK.

Aftercare: don't prune if you want to see the smoky white flower clusters in summer.

Smoke bush

more**autumn**stars

Ice plant (*Sedum spectabile*) flat-topped red flowers on a medium-sized perennial.

***Euonymus europaeus* 'Red Cascade'** red berries and leaves on a medium-sized shrub.

***Kniphofia* 'Percy's Pride'** green and yellow flower spikes on a medium-sized perennial.

Gentians (*Gentiana sino-ornata*) blue flowers on low-growing plants.

Sumach (*Rhus typhina* 'Dissecta') red and orange leaf colour on a large shrub.

winterinterest

The garden can be alive with colour, shape and form in deepest winter, so don't hibernate: put on your hat and coat and get out there.

Corkscrew hazel

(*Corylus avellana* 'Contorta')
Coiled branches that don't know which direction to grow in, yellow catkins and tiny red blooms on bare twigs all add up to a fascinating winter delight.
Height: 6m (20ft).
Spread: 6m (20ft).
Soil: well-drained soil rich in organic matter.
Light level: sun or shade for part of the day.
One season wonder?: large crinkly green leaves in spring and summer, turning yellow in autumn; winter flowers.
Local or national?: tough in all parts of the UK.
Aftercare: cut out old, non-flowering branches in spring.

Silk tassel bush (*Garrya elliptica*)

Long, slender yellow catkins cascade from plants in winter, with glossy green leaves staying fresh and perky all year round. *G. elliptica* 'James Roof' has the longest tassels.
Height: 4m (12ft).
Spread: 4m (12ft).
Soil: any; thrives in soils low in nutrients.
Light level: sunny site.
One season wonder?: evergreen leaves and winter flowers.
Local or national?: hardy if protected from cold biting winds.
Aftercare: be sure of where you want the plant to go as it dislikes being moved.

Heathers (winter-flowering *Erica* species)

Massive choice of plants with needle-like leaves and bell-shaped flowers in purple, pink or white. Choose *Erica* x *darleyensis* varieties for winter blooms.
Height: 60cm (2ft).

Corkscrew hazel

howlongwillaplantlive?

Even when grown in ideal conditions, plants have a limited lifespan. Descriptions on labels often say what this is, and here are clues as to what to expect.

Annual a plant that germinates, grows, flowers and sets seed in one growing season. Marigolds are colourful annual plants.

Biennial a plant that produces roots, stems and leaves in one growing season, flowers and sets seed in the second, and then dies. Wallflowers are a popular example of a biennial plant.

Perennial a plant that lives for at least three growing seasons. However, it is usually used in conjunction with the word herbaceous to describe a plant that dies down in autumn or winter leaving a woody stem above ground. Lupins are examples of perennials.

Shrub a plant with woody stems that is usually branched from near the base. Californian lilacs (*Ceanothus* species) are shrubs. Long lived.

Tree a woody plant that has a clear stem or trunk with a head of branches. Long lived.

Spread: 60cm (2ft).

Soil: acid, well-drained soil.

Light level: sunny.

One season wonder?: choose a number of varieties and have flowers all the year round; leaves are present twelve months of the year.

Local or national?: hardy everywhere in the UK.

Aftercare: prune lightly after flowering to keep plants compact.

Ivy (*Hedera* species)

A fantastic choice of leaf colour, shape and size is available. All species are superb as climbers or ground-cover plants, and wildlife loves them all.

Height: 5m (15ft).

Spread: 5m (15ft).

Soil: well-drained, alkaline soil.

Light level: deep shade or full sun.

One season wonder?: evergreen leaves make this a reliable and unshakable all-rounder.

Local or national?: grows throughout the UK.

Aftercare: prune in spring to control excessive growth.

Potting up When a plant grows too big for its container, it is potted up into the next size. This allows for healthy, unimpeded growth.

morewinterwonders

Helleborus argutifolius cupped green flowers on a medium-sized perennial plant.

Witch hazel (Hamamelis species) fragrant, spidery flowers on a large shrub.

Wintersweet (Chimonanthus praecox) large shrub with fragrant yellow blooms on naked branches.

Christmas box (Sarcococca confusa) highly perfumed flowers and evergreen foliage on a medium-sized shrub.

Daphne mezereum fragrant purple or pink flowers on a large shrub.

New Zealand flax

(*Phormium tenax* Purpureum Group)

Purple to rich-copper-coloured sword-like leaves and red flowers on purple-blue stems create a colour-kaleidoscope border or container.

Height: 2.5m (8ft).

Spread: 1m (3ft).

Soil: moist, well-drained soil.

Light level: full sun.

One season wonder?: evergreen, or ever-purple leaves; summer flowers.

Local or national?: wet winters can damage plants but otherwise hardy.

Aftercare: watch for, and pot up, offsets with roots that develop around the base of plants.

plants**for**health

For thousands of years plants have been at the heart of mankind's health. Their healing properties were forgotten in the race by pharmaceutical companies to develop quick-fix cures for many ailments, but over the last few years there has been a resurgence of interest in medicinal plants. It is only natural that the *Gardening Neighbours* gardens, especially Garden 5, include examples that can contribute to natural remedies for common complaints.

Maidenhair tree (*Ginkgo biloba*)

A graceful tree with green fan-shaped leaves that turn butter-yellow in autumn and fall in winter. Actually a conifer, it first appeared 190 million

Maidenhair tree

years ago and was one of the original dinosaur takeaways. This beauty has aged well. Given time, around 30 years, a sunny position and well-drained soil, plants will grow into trees 30m (100ft) tall with a 23m (75ft) spread. Its therapeutic actions have only recently been studied in the West, but have been utilized in China for centuries.

People primarily take extracts of ginkgo to help with short-term memory loss, but it is also reputed to aid depression, tinnitus, diabetes and varicose veins. Above all, it looks sensational in a garden setting.

Myrtle (*Myrtus communis*)

A beautiful evergreen plant with aromatic leaves. Highly perfumed flowers smother plants in summer and sprigs have been used in brides' bouquets for centuries. Queen Victoria made myrtle popular by including it in hers in 1840, but knowledge of myrtle's health properties goes further back. It is now commonly known that the essential oil extracted from the plant can cure chest ailments. Myrtle requires a sunny position and a well-drained soil, but can be damaged by severe winters. If your garden is exposed to winds and frost, grow it in a container that can be moved around the garden or even brought inside during periods of prolonged cold.

St John's wort (*Hypericum perforatum*)

A splendid plant with gorgeous yellow flowers throughout summer. Many nurseries label all *Hypericum* species as St John's wort, with *H.* 'Hidcote' being a popular garden choice. It retains its glossy green leaves all year round and in well-drained soil and a sunny position plants grow to 1.5m (5ft) with a similar spread. Such requirements made it the perfect choice for gardening neighbours with south-facing gardens. It's a tough plant and can withstand the coldest of winters.

Extracts are used primarily in the repair of damaged nerves, although its help in reducing

St John's wort

pain and inflammation is also well documented. Oils from the plant are used to treat circulation problems, bronchitis, sprains, bruises and gout.

French tarragon (*Artemisia dracunculus*)

A regular in the kitchen where it is used to flavour chicken, fish and rice, and is an ingredient of many sauces. French tarragon needs protection over winter and is best grown in a container, whereas its relative, Russian tarragon, is hardy but coarser leafed and not as tasty. Move containers of French tarragon to a protected area from November to March. It grows to 90cm (3ft) high with a 45cm (18in) spread and has smooth, dark green leaves.

It stimulates the digestion and is reputed to be a mild sedative. Tarragon tea is an aid for insomnia. It is also alleged to cure serpent bites, not yet a problem in the *Gardening Neighbours* gardens, and has been used to cure toothache.

Stinging nettle (*Urtica dioica*)

This requires no introduction as nettles seem to appear in places where you really could do without them. They have been around for a long time – nettle cloth has been found in Bronze Age burial sites. And when the Romans were touring Britain they brought bundles of the stinging weed and flogged themselves on the legs to keep the circulation moving during cold nights patrolling Hadrian's Wall. Didn't they have long johns in those days? Nettles were also used to produce a green dye essential to camouflage during the Second World War.

Nettles are rich in vitamin C and have been used as a spring tonic for centuries –their high iron content makes it a remarkable treatment for anaemia and poor circulation. They also have a growing reputation as a hair restorer and cure for dandruff. Nettles make great caterpillar food, an effective spray against greenfly and attract butterflies and moths in to the bargain. Leave a patch of them in your garden and see the difference they can make.

Apothecary's rose
(*Rosa gallica* var. *officinalis*)

A neat, bushy rose with stunning pinky-red blooms in summer. Plants grow to 90cm (3ft) with a similar spread when grown in well-drained soil and a sunny position. Dig in plenty of organic matter prior to planting and avoid a site that has supported roses in the past. The beauty and romance of the perfume are good enough reasons to grow this rose, but its health properties add to its attraction.

Extract of the oil is a mild sedative when used in aromatherapy, and it is claimed that preparations made from the petals of the blooms are anti-inflammatory and can also be used as an antidepressant. Rose water is mildly astringent and makes a valuable lotion for inflamed and sore eyes.

trees

Trees add maturity to an evolving garden. Their different elevations, shapes, colours and textures enable a designer to create heightened interest twelve months of the year. They are long-lived and it's therefore important to match the correct tree to your conditions.

The choice can be bewildering but, thankfully, your soil and situation will bring the list of candidates down to a manageable size.

for**clay**soil

Silver birch (*Betula pendula*): an airy, graceful tree that grows to around 8m (35ft) in a decade. The pendulous branches hang down and cast a light shade, allowing bulbs and plants to grow around the base. Silver birches look terrific in the *Gardening Neighbours* gardens where they provide welcome shade in south-facing hot spots. The shocking white trunk is the tree's trademark, and is particularly impressive in winter.

Hawthorn (*Crataegus monogyna*), flowering crab (*Malus* × *zumi* var. *calocarpa* 'Golden Hornet') and golden rain (*Laburnum* × *watereri* 'Vossii') are other trees to consider growing in clay soil.

for**sandy**soil

Honey locust (*Gleditsia triacanthos* 'Sunburst'): this has leaves that develop from a breathtaking vibrant yellow in spring to lime-green in summer, with a tantalizing glint of gold in autumn. The head of the tree is informal and open, and the leaflets ensure you always see through the canopy of foliage, making the honey locust perfect for any situation in the garden. It will grow to 6m (20ft) in a decade and is a tough customer.

Tupelo (*Nyssa sylvatica*), holm oak (*Quercus ilex*) and rowan (*Sorbus aucuparia*) are other trees to consider growing in sandy soil.

for**acid**soil

Pinus species: these are easily identified. When you spot a bundle of needle-like leaves emerging

Rowan

from a point on a branch, you know you are looking at a pine. Japanese white pine (*P. parviflora*) is a superb tree that grows no more than 3m (10ft) in a decade and is perfect for acid soil. It is low-spreading with level branches of blue and white twisted leaves and, being a conifer, bears impressive cones.

False acacia (*Robinia pseudoacacia*), tree of heaven (*Ailanthus altissima*) and Western hemlock (*Tsuga heterophylla*) are other trees to consider growing in acid soil.

for**alkaline**soil

The strawberry tree (*Arbutus unedo*): a beautiful tree that grows to 3m (10ft) in a decade. The dark green, almost black, leaves do not fall in winter and white nodding flowers shower the tree in autumn. At the same time, bright orange, strawberry-like fruits appear from the previous year's blooms. They are insipid to eat and once tried, ever forgotten. An unusual tree perfect as a specimen or in a mixed border.

European larch (*Larix decidua*), white willow (*Salix alba*) and Judas tree (*Cercis siliquastrum*) are other trees to consider growing in alkaline soil.

for**containers**

Japanese maples (*Acer palmatum* varieties): these are well suited to growing in containers, in acid composts specially prepared by manufacturers. Remember to drill drainage holes in the base of the container, water the compost mix before it dries out and feed as necessary.

Japanese maples display rich autumn hues, sensational bark colours and superb shape on patios or when they are placed in borders. Tree size depends on the size of the container: restricting the roots slows down the top growth. This is after all part of the technique used by bonsai tree growers. A partially shaded site is best and trees must be kept out of wind and early morning sunshine. Both spell danger to Japanese maples, resulting in the edges of their leaves becoming crispy and brown. For sensational colour try *A. palmatum* 'Osakazuki'.

springchoice

A century of growth from a pear tree is common, and every year the delicate white blossom breaks the heart of hardened gardeners by opening in frosty weather. The south-facing *Gardening Neighbours* gardens (numbers 5 to 8) are warm but every spring, to ensure a crop of pears, horticultural fleece will be employed on chilly nights. Drape it on trees that are growing alone, in orchards or being trained around archways. Remove the fleece in the morning when the air temperature has risen. Even without a crop of fruit, the flowers symbolize spring and a new growing year.

summerchoice

Redolent of tropical jungles, Australian tree ferns (*Dicksonia antarctica*) are not actually trees, but ferns. Their stout trunks are covered with brown hair and palm-like fronds unfurl from the apex of the trunks in spring and summer. Tree ferns can reach 10m (30ft) and can be bought in a variety of heights. In winter, prevent the crowns rotting by wrapping them with hessian or, if you are growing the trees in pots, place the containers on their sides. Stunning specimens lend an exotic air to a garden design, and the partially shaded north-facing *Gardening Neighbours* gardens (numbers 1 to 4) are perfect for strong growth. Garden 2 has examples of beautiful tree ferns.

autumnchoice

Sweet gum (*Liquidambar styraciflua* 'Lane Roberts') is arguably the best tree to grow if you want thrilling autumn colour, even better than Japanese maples – and they're good. Sweet gums grow to 5m (15ft) in a decade on soil rich in organic matter. The conical trees have large, star-like leaves of deep green. The show begins as temperature fall in autumn, with rich red and plum colours developing, sometimes as late as mid-November. Once the leaves have fallen and you have your breath back, the corky bark will entertain all winter long.

winterchoice

For the ultimate in winter attractions, grow a Tibetan cherry (*Prunus serrula*). The bark is deep mahogany on older trees, but still a gorgeous orange-brown on younger specimens. Trunks are also satin to the touch, and stroking and caressing is very much the order of the day as this smoothes the bark and increases that exquisite sheen. Plant a specimen near a path and try to resist the temptation to touch it. Best seen when all the leaves have fallen, the bark makes this tree a winter essential in moist soil, in sun or shade.

Tree fern

typesofsoil

Every gardener should get to know their garden soil as it determines whether their efforts will be successful or not. Certain plants prefer a clay soil while others prefer a sandy one. The acidity of the soil also determines how well plants grow. It is easier to match plants to your soil type than try to drastically change your soil to suit a particular plant. If you need to grow a certain plant but your soil isn't perfect, consider container gardening. You can then create the environment you or the plant want by using specially formulated compost and feeds.

classifyingyoursoil

Soil classification can be simple and, once you know what you are gardening on, buying and growing plants is easy.

Grab a handful of soil, squeeze it tight in your hand and have a look at what is formed. If you have a shiny ball of sticky soil, congratulations, you have a clay soil just like the *Gardening Neighbours*. It will waterlog in heavy rain, will retain nutrients well but bake hard in the summer sun.

If your palm is gritty and you can't form a ball of soil, well done, you have a sandy soil. It will drain freely, but will dry out quickly and lose nutrients. Both types will be improved by the addition of organic matter, and lots of it.

A mix of clay and sandy soils would form the ideal loam – a soil that drains freely but holds enough water, keeps nutrients available for roots, stays crumbly all summer and supports every kind of plant. A dream that keeps many gardeners awake at night.

Next you need to find out the acidity or alkalinity of your soil. This is measured on a pH scale. The letters pH stand for potential of

Firm soil, enriched with organic matter, around roots with your hands.
Air pockets around the roots will be the death of your plants.

Fatsia japonica *is an evergreen that needs a partially shaded, sheltered spot in any soil where plenty of organic matter has been added.*

hydrogen, which is deep into the science of biochemistry. The relevance to gardeners is that the pH affects how certain nutrients are made available to particular plants, and therefore influences growth. A reading of 7 is neutral, acidic soils are below 7 and alkaline ones are above 7.

Soil pH can be approximated by looking at the plants already growing in the soil. If you are plagued by docks, daisies and thistles, and your camellias and rhododendrons are stunning, your soil is acidic. If clover is the bane of your life and the leaves of your rhododendrons and azaleas look sickly yellow, your soil is likely to be alkaline.

Check accurately with a pH kit or meter.

plantsfor**clay**soil

Forsythia x *intermedia* varieties: a large shrub with yellow flowers covering its bare stems in early spring.

Mock orange (*Philadelphus* species): a large shrub whose white flowers fill the summer air with sweet perfume.

Flowering quince, japonica (*Chaenomeles* species): a medium-sized shrub with autumn fruits that are used in jellies and preserves.

Firethorn (*Pyracantha* species): a large shrub with red, orange or yellow berries that provide food for winter birds.

for**sandy**soil

Cotton lavender (*Santolina chamaecyparissus*): a small shrub with yellow flowers stuck on stalks from late spring to summer.

Bear's breeches (*Acanthus spinosus*): a medium-sized perennial with spires of mauve and white flowers in summer.

Clerodendrum species: fragrant blooms are followed by a crop of unusual blue berries in autumn on a large shrub.

Winter jasmine (*Jasminum nudiflorum*): in winter, fragrant yellow flowers appear on the bare branches of this medium-sized shrub, which is often used as a climbing plant.

for**acid**soil

Snowy mespilus (*Amelanchier lamarckii*): starry white flowers smother the tree in early spring.

Rhododendron species: a phenomenal range of varying sizes; many flower in summer.

Bilberry, whortleberry (*Vaccinium myrtillus*): summer flowers are followed in autumn by blue-black berries on a medium-sized shrub.

Leucothoe 'Zeblid': a small shrub whose leaves turn a beautiful bronze colour in winter.

for**alkaline**soil

Berberis darwinii: numerous orange-yellow flowers cover a medium-sized shrub in spring.

Rock rose (*Cistus* species): numerous papery flowers are produced throughout a hot summer on a small shrub.

Chaste tree (*Vitex agnus-castus*): fragrant violet-blue flowers appear in autumn on a large shrub.

Photinia x *fraseri* 'Red Robin': a large shrub with high-gloss leaves, red when young, that are a constant joy throughout winter.

buyingplants

Visiting a nursery or website to buy plants is one of the most enjoyable apects of gardening. It can also be one of the most expensive as it's virtually impossible to be strong-willed when faced with floriferous temptations.

Before venturing out make a list of the plants you need. This way you will return home with at least something that fits into your garden design. If you know that making a list and sticking to it isn't your forte, stagger your visits to retailers over the year. This way you will avoid the common practice of buying all your plants during one fine day in spring when most of them are in flower. They may look good for a week or two but they will hardly provide that year-round-interest garden you promised yourself. After all, do you buy all your clothes in one mad weekend in April? Exactly.

It's always worth asking gardening friends about the plant retailers in your area. Most of them will have a tale or two about their favourites and not so favourites. If possible, visit a nursery or garden centre when they have just had a fresh delivery of plants and be the first to select the best. If this is midweek then all the better, as weekends get crowded and knowledgeable staff may be too busy to answer your queries.

Wherever possible, get your hands on plants before you buy them. Then follow these guidelines to make sure they are in the best possible condition – and will stay that way until you plant them.

● Look for signs of pests and diseases. Check the undersides of leaves for damage. If you are feeling public-spirited point out poor plants to retailers' assistants.

(above) Check plants if they are delivered to your garden.

(opposite) Remove plants from pots and check for healthy white roots.

goodplant,**bad**plant

good roots show through the drainage holes in the container.
 bad no roots show through the container drainage holes or they are tightly coiled around the base of the pot.

good the surface of the compost is free of weeds and moss.
 bad the surface of compost is covered by a dense growth of weeds or moss.

good pots are clean, well labelled.
 bad pots are cracked or broken with no label.

good healthy growth with no signs of pests or diseases.
 bad damage to leaves and roots; look out for notches in leaves as an indication of possible vine-weevil damage.

good plants in packets show healthy buds and no white roots.
 bad plants in packets have spindly shoot- and root-growth.

the compost and turn the pot over. Roots should just be appearing through the drainage holes. This means the plant has rooted all the way through the compost and will grow away quickly once it's in your garden. Roots that have coiled around the base of the pot usually mean that the plant has been in the container for a long time and could be suffering.

Ease the pot off the roots and compost. The compost should cling to the roots to form a solid root-ball, and should be evenly moist, neither waterlogged or dry. There are exceptions to this guideline – for example when buying aquatic plants or ones that require desert-like conditions.

> **'If the plant is working hard and is appropriate for the space then it's a worthy plant'**
> *Chris Beardshaw*

- It isn't fair to the retailer or the plant to rip a root ball to pieces, but do have a close look at the outer surface. You may see small, spherical objects that look like insect eggs. They are in fact pellets of fertilizer and have been included in the compost mix to ensure the vitality of the plant.

If you are happy with all your checks go ahead and buy the plant. Keep the receipt as most retailers will consider a complaint if you can produce it, even when the plant is a couple of years old.

- Avoid buying plants and leaving them in a hot car for hours before returning home. They can lose a tremendous amount of water and may never recover.

- Water all plants a day before planting them.

Finally, if you are buying by mail order or via the Internet, unwrap all the plants as soon as you receive them and check for quality and signs of deterioration.

- Look for a thick layer of moss or liverwort on the surface of the compost. If present, it indicates that the plant has been in the pot for a long time and has not been treated to top dressing or quality care. The same goes for weeds growing from the compost. They will be competing, and probably winning, a battle with the plant for available water and nutrients. It's best to avoid buying such moss- or weed-infested plants.

- Ask staff if you can inspect the roots of trees and shrubs. A retailer selling top-quality stock will welcome such inspection – in a part of his premises where any falling compost can be cleared up. Place your hand on the surface of

howto**plant**

planting**in**a**border**

Preparing the soil is vital to the longevity of your plants. The most expensive specimen will deteriorate in poor soil so add plenty of organic matter and general fertilizer a month before planting. Only consider doing this when the soil is moist but not wet. If it sticks to your gardening boots you should leave planting for another day. However, if the soil in your garden is heavy clay you may just have to go ahead when time allows. Container-grown plants will sit happily in their pots until conditions are perfect. Remember to check and water them every day.

1 Dig a hole 10cm (4in) deeper and wider than the pot your plant is growing in and place a layer of compost or organic matter in the base of the hole. Incorporate a spadeful of the same organic matter in the excavated soil.

2 Put the pot, still containing the plant, in the hole. The top of the pot should be level with the top of the hole.

Sometimes pots have to be cut off vigorous root systems.

'Establishing plants in odd numbers tends to create a more informal, naturalistic appearance in the garden than plants used either as individuals or in even numbers where the appearance can be more contrived or formal'
Chris Beardshaw

3 Take the pot out of the hole and place your hand over the surface of the compost. Turn the plant upside down. The pot may slide off gracefully revealing a compact rootball. If nothing happens, you will need to gently tap the edge of the pot. A tender squeeze around the middle of the pot usually has the most stubborn plants out in a flash. If the plant still refuses to budge, place it the right way up on the ground and carefully cut the pot off the root ball. Watering the day before planting usually prevents the need for such drastic action.

4 Carefully sit the plant on the layer of organic matter in the base of the planting hole.

5 Check that the surface of the compost is the same as the lip of the hole. Either add or remove organic matter from the layer in the base of the hole to adjust the height of the plant.

6 Ease and tease entwined roots from around the root ball.

7 Fill the space between the root ball and the sides of the hole with the mixture of excavated soil and organic matter. As the space is filled, firm the mix down with your hands. Fill and firm until the levels are equal. Firm again using your heel, gently holding any trailing branches away from the soil and foot.

8 Water the plant. This will wash and settle the soil around the roots. The soil may need topping up to ensure that the plant is stable and

do's**&**don'ts

✔ **do** water container-grown plants before and after planting.

✘ **don't** break up the root ball.

✔ **do** firm in plants in borders with your hands and a well-heeled boot.

✘ **don't** try to remove a plant from its pot by pulling at the shoots.

✔ **do** check plants after frosty weather, which can lift newly planted specimens out of the soil.

✘ **don't** forget to label your plants or make a note of their names.

✔ **do** put any supports or tree stakes into the soil before planting to avoid damage to roots.

✘ **don't** use containers without drainage holes, unless you are planting up aquatic plants.

✔ **do** wear eye protectors and gloves when drilling pots. If you're unsure of your skills, buy containers with pre-drilled drainage holes.

✘ **don't** strain your back carrying containers. Make or buy a set of wheels to move larger ones around a patio.

✔ **do** buy frost-proof containers.

all the roots are covered. Check the soil level immediately the water has soaked away and again a couple of days later.

9 Keep the plant well watered even when light rain has fallen. The roots will soon develop in soil rich in organic matter.

If you are planting a bare-root plant with no soil around its roots, spread the roots on the layer of organic matter in the base of the planting hole. Look for the darker area on the stem. This is the level to which the plant must be planted. Bare-root roses are a popular buy in autumn along with many trees and shrubs. When buying plants in boxes or strips, carefully remove the containers – never pull at the plants – and check for the presence of heathly, white roots.

planting**in**a**container**

Anything can grow in a container given water, food, the correct compost and drainage holes. And there are so many types of container that the hardest part is choosing the correct one for your patio or to stand in your border. Once you've decided, and the choice is personal, ensure that the container has drainage holes in its base. This is essential as only aquatic plants will tolerate constant water at their roots. Some cheaper terracotta pots do not have drainage holes so use a small, sharp masonry bit to drill three small holes in close proximity to each other. Once these are drilled, merge them into one with a larger drill bit.

1 Place a piece of fine mesh or chicken netting inside the pot to cover the base. This stops slugs, snails and other unwanted visitors crawling into your pot.

2 Place a layer of terracotta shards on the netting. These can be bought from enterprising garden retailers, or you can carefully break a few cheap pots. The shards help drainage but, more importantly, they stop compost washing through the drainage holes all over your clean patio. The depth of the layer depends on the size of the pot. For a 30cm (12in) diameter container it should be 5cm (2in) deep. An alternative to terracotta shards are chunks of polystyrene. They do the same job but are lighter and easier to handle.

3 Part fill the container with your preferred compost mix.

4 Remove the plants from their pots, place them on the compost and fill in the gaps between them with more compost. The final level of compost should be 5cm (2 in) below the rim of a 30cm (12in) container.

5 Firm around all plants with your hands, water the container and top up the compost levels as required.

> 'If you were to plant in groups of even numbers, your brain would automatically separate the group into its component parts, whereas drifts of odd numbers are seen as one large group, giving a much more soft and flowing look to your border'
> *Ali Ward*

How many people does it take to fill a Cretan urn? Firm compost down in all shapes of container to remove air pockets.

organic**matter**

Organic matter is an essential ingredient in successful gardening. Used in planting mixtures, potting composts and mulches, it is the foundation of great gardens. It helps to hold the sticky particles of a clay soil apart – lorry loads of organic matter were added to the *Gardening Neighbours* gardens to improve drainage – and will also add bulk to a light sandy soil. Either dig organic matter into the soil or spread it on the surface to act as a weed-suppressing blanket. Whatever your soil, it needs organic matter, and it can't get enough of it.

Manures: All animal manures are wonderful for the garden but they have to be well-rotted before use. The bacteria that rot them down use nitrogen in the process and if fresh manure is applied to soil they will use up all this valuable nutrient, leaving none for the plants. Well-rotted horse manure containing small amounts of straw is perfect for adding to planting holes and to use as mulches. It should be dark brown and crumbly, with no distasteful smell. Pile up fresh manure and allow it to rot down for a year before use. Check local farms for availability.

container**seasons**

spring Plant up containers but if you're buying plants for them make sure they are hardy or prepared for any cold spells. If not, keep the planted container in a light, frost-free position until the temperature rises.

summer Water, feed and deadhead plants to keep a display pulsing through the hot months.

autumn Stop feeding plants. Replace any faded summer bedding plants with autumn bloomers or shrubs.

winter Wrap frost-tender pots in bubble insulation to protect them and prevent roots freezing. Plants can be wrapped in horticultural fleece or 'wrapped in a roll of cardboard stuffed with straw to protect them from the worst of the cold', says Ali Ward. If pots are too heavy to lift, 'they too can be wrapped and take their chances outside', she advises. Add colour with winter-flowering bedding plants such as pansies.

Spent mushroom compost: Mushroom farms discard their growing medium when it is exhausted of nutrients. It is already composted and is an ideal mulch. Don't use it around acid-loving plants such as camellias and heather as it contains chalk, which increases the alkaline value of the soil. And don't use it in conjunction with manures as gases that can harm plants are released when the two are mixed. Some mushroom compost may contain traces of insecticide used in production of the crop. Check business directories for details of your local mushroom farm.

Home-made compost: The best way to garden. A compost bin is easily made or purchased and will utilize all the green waste in your garden and kitchen. One compost bin will not be enough.

Banana skins: Place a banana skin in every planting hole and provide, on a small but useful scale, organic matter and nutrient additives.

Peat: The great debate in gardening is whether to use peat. Manufacturers say they use sympathetic methods to farm it but many environmentalists are concerned at the way peat bogs are disappearing. The alternatives are good and readily available. Coir, based on coconut fibre, is now the main constituent of many proprietary soil improvers and does a wonderful job.

Manufactured planting and mulching mixtures: These are good quality, but expensive compared to home-made compost. They usually contain added chemical nutrients so be careful if you are gardening organically. The mixtures are available from all garden retailers in an assortment of sizes. Take care when lifting the sacks as they are often heavy, and never buy bags saturated with water as nutrients will have been washed out.

Dig in organic matter, bought or home-made, to ensure the success of your plants.

home-made**compost**

If you pile all your prunings, grass clippings and vegetable waste into a dark, wet corner of the garden and expect to produce rich, crumbly compost, you are going to be bitterly disappointed. However, it is easy to make glorious compost if you follow a few guidelines.

- Choose a highly insulated compost bin, with a lid, that complements your garden

border**seasons**

spring Traditionally the time for planting trees and shrubs, due to warm soil and pleasant working conditions. Mulch damp soil with a thick layer of organic matter to retain moisture, just in case the summer is hot and dry.

summer Water plants when they become dry. Watch out for pests and control them. Plant container-grown plants – this can be done all year round.

autumn If you don't mind the unkempt look, leave flower heads to set and distribute seed. Plant bare-root roses and trees in well-prepared soil. Bring tender plants under cover before frosts cause damage.

winter Plant winter-flowering shrubs if the soil hasn't frozen solid. Wrap hessian around frost-sensitive pots in the border to prevent cracking and flaking.

surroundings. Ready-made types can be bought from garden retailers, or you can build one yourself from brick or wood.

- Stand the bin directly on the soil in a semi-shaded place out of direct rain. Bacteria will break down the vegetable matter you put in the bin, and if you look after them they will reward you with unstinting work. Bacteria like it warm and not too wet, and live naturally in the soil on leaves, grass clippings and everything you plan to put in the bin.
- Add organic matter to the bin in 15cm (6in) layers, putting a 5cm (2in) layer of garden soil between each one. The soil will provide extra bacteria for the process.
- Keep the carbon and nitrogen ratio balanced for best results. Grass clippings are rich in nitrogen whereas straw, sawdust and leaves are rich in carbon. If you are putting lots of grass clippings in the bin, counter them with straw or leaves. Do this within each layer to avoid any one layer containing 100 per cent of any one material.
- Keep the lid on the compost bin to retain heat whenever possible.
- When the compost bin is full leave it alone for five to six months.
- Then enjoy using your home-made compost all around the garden.

caring**for**plants

water

Every plant needs water to survive and it's rare for rain to supply 100 per cent of its requirements through the year. Whether you use a watering can, hosepipe, sprinkler or buckets of used bath water, it is best to give plants a thorough soaking. This encourages deep rooting and saves the time spent on frequent watering.

Once water is in the soil or compost, much of it is lost through evaporation back into the air. Reduce this water loss by applying a thick covering of organic matter or pebbles, known as a mulch, to the surface. Bark chippings look good; homemade compost adds exceptional organic matter to the soil as it breaks down; and well-rotted manure helps to improve the structure of soil. All mulches also reduce weed growth. They have to be 10cm (4in) thick to be effective and must only be applied to wet soil. On dry soils they will stop rain water penetrating. Worms and movement in the soil will reduce the thickness of the mulch over a year, so top up levels when required.

Bark chippings help to reduce water loss.

In an average year more than 150,000 litres (30,000 gallons) of rain falls on an average-sized roof in the UK. Collect as much of this as you can in a water butt placed at the base of a drainpipe. Raise the butt off the ground to allow easy access with a watering can.

Recycled or grey water refers to used water from bathrooms and kitchens. The water itself is perfectly safe for the garden – the only concern is the type and strength of detergents that have been added to it. Bath water is generally great for plants as the gentle soaps present can actually benefit them – greenfly are susceptible to a foaming with soap. Grey water from dishwashers and washing machines may contain strong detergents, even bleaching agents, that could cause damage. Read the information on the relevant packaging before pouring grey water on the soil and over plants.

do's**&**don'ts

✔ **do** water plants before they wilt.

✘ **don't** wait until evening to water a wilted plant. Water immediately.

✔ **do** wait until evening if it isn't an emergency.

✘ **don't** follow a little and often policy.

✔ **do** give plants a drenching.

✘ **don't** use sprinklers and hosepipes without getting permission from your local council.

✔ **do** mulch wet soil to conserve water.

✘ **don't** mulch dry soil as this will stop water penetrating the surface.

✔ **do** collect water in a water butt.

✘ **don't** spray leaves in hot weather.

✔ **do** water the soil around plants. This gets water to where it is needed – the roots.

food

Plants need food to survive and thrive. The soil provides this but, as more and more plants are cultivated, it becomes exhausted and lacking in nutrients. It is up to the gardener to put these back. Plants require large amounts of three major plant nutrients.

- Nitrogen is responsible for healthy leaf growth. If a plant is lacking in nitrogen its leaves will be small and sickly.
- Phosphates are responsible for healthy root

growth. If a plant is lacking in phosphates its roots will be stunted and its leaves will have a telltale purplish tinge.

- Potash is responsible for healthy flowers and fruit. If a plant is lacking in phosphates the flowers will be smaller than usual, lacking in colour and fruit yield will be low.

General fertilizers contain all these nutrients and somewhere on the packaging the manufacturer has to state the percentage of each type. This is expressed as three figures, nitrogen being the first, phosphates the second and potash the third. For example, the packaging for a lawn fertilizer could state 40:10:1, meaning that there is lots of nitrogen to green up the leaves, a little bit of phosphate to support some root growth and little emphasis on potash for fruit or flower development. You're greening up the lawn remember, so who needs phosphates? A feed specifically designed for tomatoes will have a higher percentage of potash because a heavy crop is required. Look for high percentages of a particular nutrient if your plants have a specific problem.

A balanced fertilizer contains equal percentages of each of the three main nutrients, 7:7:7 for example. This is a general, balanced fertilizer and is perfect for scattering on the soil before planting to get plants off to a flying start.

Gardeners also have a choice between organic and inorganic fertilizers. Organic ones are derived from animals or vegetables and are slow-acting in the soil. They supply plants with a steady supply of food over a long period of time. Inorganic fertilizers are fast-acting and give plants a quick boost, sometimes taking effect within two days.

Before applying any fertilizer check the levels in the soil. Kits are available from graden retailers which are easy to use and give results in minutes. They could save time, money and your plants. When taking soil samples for the kit, do so from different areas of the garden for an accurate picture of soil mineral levels.

do's&don'ts

✓ **do** study your plants for signs of nutrient deficiency.

✗ **don't** feed them unless they are lacking a nutrient.

✓ **do** check your soil with a plant nutrient test kit.

✗ **don't** apply fertilizers in dry weather.

✓ **do** water all fertilizers into the soil.

✗ **don't** put a fertilizer directly on leaves unless it is labelled as being a foliar feed.

✓ **do** apply only the recommended quantities of fertilizer.

✗ **don't** store bags of fertilizer in damp areas.

✓ **do** buy only the amount of fertilizer you will need for a season at any one time.

✗ **don't** neglect adding organic matter because you think fertilizers will do the job.

✓ **do** read packaging carefully to ensure that a fertilizer is the one you need.

Get children involved in all aspects of gardening, and allow a little adventure into your garden.

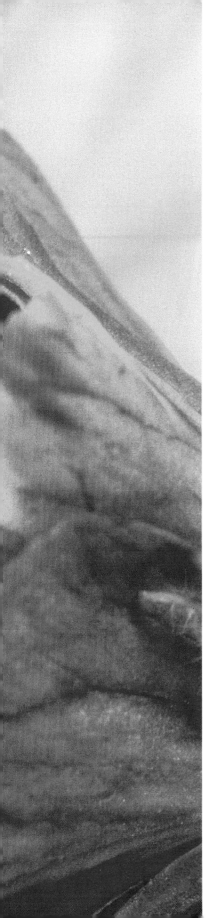

chapter**five**

wildlife

wildlife *n*. wild animals and plants collectively:
a term used esp. of fauna

local wildlife perks up the moment a spade is thrust into yielding soil, and as the gardening neighbours set to work the sound of beaks being sharpened, wings being stretched and the gentle shuffle of paws and claws could be heard. Gardening is far from being a solitary experience. Do absolutely nothing in your garden and wildlife will still find your plot. Give it the slightest of helpful nudges and it will become a wondrous balance of ecosystems.

Garden 8 was created to be irresistible to wildlife, with Ali's design incorporating a fantastic and ecologically rich pond. But every one of the eight gardens will be equally irresistible, whether their owners like it or not. The beautiful yellow flowers in Garden 5 will attract a multitude of butterflies, hoverflies and insects, and the massed planting of ground-cover plants in Garden 2 provides ideal cover for animals and birds.

Chris and Ali's designs prove that a wildlife garden doesn't have to be a field of corn liberally sprinkled with the gentle nodding heads of ephemeral poppies. Neither does it have to look like a rundown scrap of wasteland choking at the foundations of an otherwise orderly neighbourhood. Chris Beardshaw says that 'its what you do in the space that is important and the way in which you link your site with the surroundings to create a staging post for the wildlife'. A wildlife garden can look just the way you want it to look, be it large, small, wild or tamed.

'Size is not important in the creation of an effective habitat for wildlife' *Chris Beardshaw*

attracting**wildlife**

The *Gardening Neighbours* gardens bristle with ideas designed to attract wildlife, and if you want to create a garden that is a magnet for frogs, toads, newts and birds, try some of the following.

food

Plants will provide most of the food for wildlife in a garden, with berries on trees and shrubs supplying essential meals in autumn and winter. Additional sustenance will get the crowds flocking in to your wildlife restaurant. Bird tables are easy to make and are also a popular purchase. Ensure that a table is over 1.5m (5ft) high to allow birds to feed in peace without having to keep a watchful eye out for cats. Make sure it has a rim all around the edge to help retain seed and food during feeding times. Position the table away from walls and other predator-pouncing areas.

Squirrels can provide hours of fun when they raid the bird table. You can either welcome these visitors into your garden and accept that they will steal some of the food put out for birds, or try and combat their forays into bird territory. Put all seed and food in bird feeders that are deemed to be squirrel proof.

shelter

Providing shelter for wildlife is a sure way to encourage long-term visits. Pile up logs or thick prunings in the shady spots of your flower borders. Even better, design a low retaining wall or feature that uses wood. The wood will eventually rot down and provide a fun-filled wildlife playground. Insects, worms and woodlice also need this decaying organic material for survival. The rarely seen stag beetle procreates in dead and rotting wood. Perhaps it would be more commonplace if it changed its reproductive *modus operandi*.

Leaving tree stumps in the ground will encourage a multitude of insects and fungi to rendezvous in your garden. Some of the incoming fungi may be troublesome to border plants and trees, and one or two may even cause toadstools to pop up in your lawn. How far you go with attracting and retaining wildlife is obviously a personal choice, but the unwanted side effects of encouraging it, such as slight blemishing of your lawn, are easily controlled.

Bare brick walls can support wildlife if you retain all the nooks and crannies. Solitary bees will thank you for this, individually of course. It's not difficult to imagine the different populations of insects, animals and reptiles living in dry stone walls, another feature worth considering in a garden design.

Clothe a wall with plant life and you have instantly created a wildlife haven. The covering of ivy foliage acts as a spider's duvet, an eider-down for small birds and perhaps a continental quilt for a dormouse or two. The wattle fencing panels in Garden 8 not only look spectacular, but provide shelter for lots of wildlife. Insects will scurry behind the layered hazel, fungi will grow on the wood – and the fencing stops the wind from howling through exposed gardens.

a**bed**for**the**night

Encourage birds to nest in your garden and enjoy guaranteed wildlife activity all year round. Trees will help to supply nesting materials and nesting boxes are an ideal encouragement for birds. Place the boxes out of direct sunlight to protect eggs and fledglings, and avoid areas like overhanging branches and roofs which may give predators the chance to attack.

There are different types of boxes for the numerous birds looking for a home. Nuthatches and tits will choose one with an entrance of 28mm (just over an inch), whereas house sparrows prefer a larger front door at 32mm (1¼in). Boxes with open fronts attract robins, and a larger version high in a tree may just attract an owl or kestrel.

The luxuriant foliage around the pond in garden 8 will provide shade and protection for wildlife.

water**for**wildlife

A wildlife pond is the most natural and easily constructed water feature. Choose a semi-shaded site away from areas of high garden activity and preferably away from overhanging trees. Falling leaves will rot in the pond and turn the water acidic. Making a well-balanced wildlife pond is easy and has wide-ranging rewards.

1 Trace the shape of the pond on the soil surface to suit your design and when you are happy with this, dig. Use planks of wood and a spirit level to check the final level. The depth of pond isn't as crucial as the gradient, or beach area, leading into the water.

2 Gently slope the sides of the pond towards the deepest part of the water, which should ideally be 60cm (2ft). This allows birds to have a comfortable bath in the shallow end, hedge-hogs and other animals to slowly escape any unexpected falls and makes a frog's life so much easier.

3 Now fit a plastic or butyl liner. First remove all stones and roots that might puncture it,

(above) A well placed rock in Garden 2 will provide welcome shade for wildlife – and looks terrific.

(top) Gentle bubbles will help oxygenate a pool, preventing algae growth and keeping everything crystal clear in Garden 8.

(opposite) Provide a gently shelving beach area into wildlife ponds to help bugs and beasties get in and out safely.

then smooth a 5cm (2in) layer of sand onto the dug surface and fit the liner in place. Make sure there is plenty of spare liner around the lip of the hole.

4 Place a 10cm (4in) layer of excavated soil in the bottom of the pond. Don't use fertile topsoil as any nutrients that it contains would be detrimental to pond life. Pass the soil through a garden riddle to remove anything that may puncture the lining. A great idea is to persuade a friend with an established pond to donate a couple of spadefuls of silt from their wildlife haven. This will immediately introduce millions of micro-organisms to your pond.

5 Gently trickle water into the pond. The liner will mould itself to the shape of the hole. When the pond is full allow the water to stand for three days before planting. This allows any chlorine present to evaporate and the soil to settle.

6 Cover any visible liner near the edges of the pond with pebbles or stones. Offcuts of timber cladding from the hazel fencing were used for the pond in Garden 8 to ensure a natural look in keeping with the overall design of the garden. Pebbles can also be used to great effect.

7 Introduce your chosen plants and leave your pond to exert its hypnotic charm on the local wildlife.

If the thought of all that digging is too much, a mini-pond can be created in a half barrel. These barrels come in a variety of sizes but one with a diameter of 45cm (1ft 6in) will be most suitable. Barrels are generally stored outside covered areas in garden centres and consequently collect rain water. Look for one that's full of water as this will guarantee its water-holding capabilities. All barrels can be lined with black plastic to ensure a watertight finish.

The only thing to remember when planting up a barrel is to place it in its final position before filling it with water and plants. Even a small barrel is heavy when full. Otherwise it's as simple as filling the barrel with water and suitable plants, and enjoying the wildlife. Group different-sized barrels together to form a wonderful display and an even greater incentive for visitors from the wild.

If your garden is too small, or you have young children who may find the fascination of any depth of water too much of a temptation, a bird bath will provide welcome water for birds. This reduces the dangers to children but still encourages wildlife. Make sure the baths are secure and won't topple over, and change the water every day to prevent a build-up of debris. Simple ideas like an upturned dustbin lid filled with water will also offer birds a welcome drink.

plantsforawildlifepond

Many ferns grow beautifully in the damp soil surrounding a pond and provide evergreen cover for insects and reptiles. Don't be put off by the names, they're only showing off.

Polystichum setiferum **Divisilobum Group** keeps most of its soft-textured, finely divided fronds all the year round. It grows 60cm (2ft) high and wide.

Polystichum aculeatum **'Pulcherrimum'** has dainty fronds that are light green in spring and darken in summer. Plants grow 60cm (2ft) high and wide.

Dryopteris filix-mas, the impressive male fern, retains some of its arching, mid-green fronds all year round if grown in the shade. These also provide extra shade for surrounding plants as they grow to 1.2m (4ft) high and 1m (3ft) wide.

Plantain lilies (*Hosta* varieties) are planted around much of the water in the *Gardening Neighbours* gardens. There is such a variety of leaf shape, colour and texture that they are invaluable for softening the edge of a pond or providing shelter and landing platforms for insects. The leaves can be anything from slender arrows to wide, six-lane highways and their colours range through all

(above) Dense leaf growth around ponds provides shelter and shade for wildlife. Check that leaves don't fall in and pollute the water in autumn.

(opposite) Hostas have luxuriant leaves and will shade wildlife on sunny days. They will also attract slugs and snails.

slugs**and**snails

Slugs and snails don't have to be garden enemy number one, especially in a balanced wildlife garden. There are ways and means of dealing with them without resorting to chemicals (see page 104).

possible shades of green into the blues, with striped variegations in the mix. As if that wasn't enough, many varieties produce graceful spikes of purple flowers in summer. They need the moist soil and semi-shaded conditions around a wildlife pond. Hostas are sitting targets for voracious slugs and snails, but *H.* 'Sum and Substance' is often ignored by molluscs. It can also tolerate a sunny position.

Iris laevigata **'Variegata'**, the variegated Japanese water iris, is a must-grow pond plant. The white-and-green striped leaves are present all year round and two flushes of its blue flowers are very often possible, one in early summer with another in autumn. Place baskets containing clumps of the plants in the shallow beach section of the pond to provide a physical and visual transition from border to water. Wildlife will nibble at the plant's roots and its 60cm (2ft) high leaves will provide shade on hot days.

Zebra rush (and check out this botanical name, *Schoenoplectus lacustris* subsp. *tabernaemontani* 'Zebrinus') is, despite its name, a simple rush with horizontal bands of white on green leafless stems. It spreads all over the place and grows to 1.5m (5ft) high. This heavyweight player is best suited to a larger pond.

Arum lily (*Zantedeschia aethiopica* 'Crow-borough') is a tropical-looking plant which grows from a bulb, and is at home in the murky shallows of a wildlife pond. The juicy, dark green leaves form large clumps from which striking white flowers emerge. Wildlife adores the shade they offer and the flowers provide a sensational eye-catching display.

awildlife**border**

Mahonia × *media* **'Lionel Fortescue'** has bright yellow racemes that cascade from a central growing point and look breathtaking in the depths of winter. The blue-black berries that follow are a tasty treat for the early birds of spring. Any soil will support healthy growth that eventually reaches 6m (20ft) high and wide. Pruning in April, once the birds have feasted and moved to other feeding stations, will keep everything under control. The spiky, evergreen leaves provide shelter for birds and other wildlife foraging in frozen conditions.

Lilacs (*Syringa vulgaris*) can be anything but vulgar, with white, rose, red and lavender flowers all becoming popular. Birds, butterflies, bees and gardeners all love the large, strongly scented blooms that appear in May and June. In sunny positions and on any soil, expect most lilacs to grow into trees 5m (15ft) high. If any straggly branches develop, often a criticism of lilacs, cut them out when flowering has finished.

Butterfly bush (*Buddleja davidii* varieties) must be the most aptly named of all plants. Whichever variety you choose, be it 'Royal Red', 'White Profusion' or 'Empire Blue', you can guarantee that clouds of frenzied butterflies will descend on your garden in late summer. They can't resist the cone-shaped flower clusters on shrubs 5m (15ft) high. All the plant requires is a well-drained soil and a sunny position. If left to do its own thing, it

Mahonia × *media*

will grow into an untidy specimen with flowers at the very top of each spindly branch – a mere floral speck in the far distance. In March, it is far better to prune the previous year's growth to 10cm (4in) of old wood. Last year's growth is lighter in colour than older wood. This helps to contain the plant and to produce strong compact growth and fantastic flowers. It also means that everyone can share in the enjoyment of the butterflies at a manageable height.

Russian sage

Russian sage (*Perovskia atriplicifolia* 'Blue Spire') has violet-blue flowers in late summer – and it's not only gardeners who enjoy them. Bees can't resist a closer look. The flowers are produced on grey-white spikes above slender, aromatic leaves. If left unattended, Russian sage grows to 1.5m (5ft) high with a similar spread. It does insist on well-drained soil and a sunny position. In spring, cut every branch to 30cm (12in) above ground level. This ensures that the plant will retain a compact shape and produce plenty of first-class blooms.

Veronica (*Hebe* varieties) comes in all shapes, sizes and colours, but all varieties attract birds and butterflies into the wildlife garden. Veronicas require a well-drained soil in a partially shaded position, and some protection from bitingly cold winters. When choosing varieties at a garden retailer, remember that the larger the leaf the more tender the plant. *H.* 'Autumn Glory' is a favourite because of its long flowering season and the way it stands up to cold weather. Purple flowers are produced from June until November on plants that grow to 1.5m (5ft) high and wide.

Veronica

environmentally**friendly**

Wildlife will flourish in a pesticide-free garden. Of course, wildlife includes slugs and greenfly but, as the balance of the garden establishes, these unwanted guests will actually diminish in number. That is because their natural predators will increase. Clever stuff, where everyone and everything wins except the slugs and greenfly.

It is an easy option to turn to chemical warfare, using an arsenal of toxic sprays to quickly kill all pests. Ready-mixed pesticides, fungicides and herbicides are all waiting for trigger-happy gardeners to start the carnage. And when you see the damage that can occur in a garden overnight it is tempting to reach for the spray. The problem is that, on the way to wiping out the enemy, many chemicals also kill the good guys, the natural predators. Sometimes this happens indirectly. Slug pellets do a great job in attracting and then killing slugs. A battlefield littered with dead bodies is evidence enough. However, the chemicals inside the dead slugs could be ingested by a frog or bird in search of a juicy treat. The chemical then travels through the food chain causing damage every step of the way.

If you want an environmentally friendly garden, follow these guidelines – and be patient. A pesticide-free garden allows nature to find a balance between the hunters and the hunted.

- If you kill all the greenfly with chemical sprays birds, in particular blue tits, will have nothing to feed on and will go elsewhere in search of a live meal. It's good wildlife practice to encourage them to feed around plants infested with greenfly by hanging feeders nearby. They will enjoy the food you provide and then move greedily on to the plants, stripping them of their unwanted pests.

- Encourage wildlife by making your own compost from the vegetation in the garden. Purpose-made compost bins are available and swallow up masses of leaves, grass clippings and precious vegetable waste from the kitchen. Without a bin all that valuable resource would disappear in council-run refuse sites. Ones that stand directly on the soil are irresistible to wildlife, with many a hedgehog setting up a cosy residence in the base of a bin.

- Sweep fallen leaves up from the lawn and bag them in black plastic sacks, then leave the sacks in a quiet corner for a year. The leaves will rot down to form leaf mould, a crumbly additive for compost or mulch for your special plants. Rake leaves that have fallen onto borders into small piles. Animals and insects will use them for shelter and as nesting sites.

- Let weeds and debris that you clear from your pond lie at the side of the water for a day. This

natural**slug**control

- To keep the slug population down to manageable numbers the natural way, ensure that your wildlife pond is thriving and that birds visit your garden.

- Introduce nematodes to control slugs biologically. These microscopic worms get under the surface of the slug, multiply and kill it from inside its own body. More nematodes are then released into the soil to infect more slugs. They are harmless to everything else in the soil, and do no harm to birds and humans. Nematodes are available from most garden retailers.

- Put a mulch or a covering of gravel or crushed eggshells around slug-susceptible plants. This will scratch at the slugs' undersides, making it too uncomfortable for them to persist in attacks.

- Bury containers of beer in the soil around plants. Leave a 1cm (½in) lip above soil level. Slugs will be attracted to the smell and will fall into the containers and drown.

will allow any beasties to scamper back into their watery habitats.

- Avoid the temptation to clip, snip and tidy up old flower heads. Birds feed on many of the seeds that are quietly developing on the plants.
- Ask where stone products come from before buying, and follow the gardening neighbours' example by making full use of reconstituted stone or concrete as opposed to slabs torn from precious limestone pavements. Natural sources of limestone are disappearing and consequently wildlife is losing vital and irreplaceable habitats.
- Wild species belong in the wild. Collect your plants from garden centres and nurseries, and always check labels to ensure they are from cultivated, not wild, stock.
- Frog spawn, and for that matter frogs, also belong in the wild. Never import frog spawn from a natural pond. Rest assured that, given time, frogs will find your pond.

Gardeners can influence wildlife beyond their own garden fences. The use of peat is a hotly debated subject. It takes thousands of years to form and isn't necessary in gardens. Many people consider that digging it out and incorporating it in compost is wasteful, as it isn't essential and there are outstanding alternatives that have undergone rigorous testing, analysis and improvement. Coir, based on coconut fibre, and composted bark are both excellent substitutes.

Peat bogs are needed by wildlife. Destroy them and the creatures that rely on them will decline – it's an easy equation. But it's really up to gardeners to make up their own minds about whether they use peat in compost and mulches.

chapter**six**

gardening for children

child *n., pl.* **children**. a boy or girl between birth and puberty.

ali's design for Garden 7 is fun, child-friendly and looks terrific. Like most gardeners, the gardening neighbours don't have the space to devote vast areas to children. Therefore, a garden needs to be multifunctional, catering for young explorers and adults alike.

A garden can exert strong influences on a child's education. It can be a place in which to play, learn and develop skills, in the security of familiar surroundings. A well designed garden is a terrifically stimulating teaching aid. Numbers, colours, shapes and textures will graduate to gardening skills and achievements. Safety is paramount but it shouldn't be so overpowering as to inhibit development and discovery. Children need to learn about danger in a controlled and risk-free environment. Getting a child-friendly garden right is therefore a wonderful achievement with rich rewards for the future. Above all, where else can a five-year-old get covered in soil from head to toe and be praised for it?

Begin to help children appreciate a garden, and importantly their part in it, and the next generation of gardening neighbours will develop. Gardens can be fun, as Ali's design and implementation proves, and as the children in garden 7 will testify to, day after day, month after month, and year after year.

gardens**to**play**in**

Make a garden an exciting playground and children will plead to leave the television and computer screens in order to play outside. Reaching a balance between theme park and garden is vital to a successful design, but there is no escaping the fact that most children consider garishly coloured play-equipment essential. Sandpits can be bought in the shapes of boats and animals. Trampolines, buckets and miniature tables and chairs all add up to hours of enjoyment, badminton nets and football posts are essential for further

developing the Olympic spirit, but the ultimate achievement for many upwardly mobile children is a place they can call their own. Somewhere they can relax after a hard morning at playschool, somewhere to chill out and contemplate their homework, somewhere to entertain their teddy bears and friends.

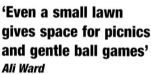

The lawn will get a lot of use and provides a safe landing for falls and jumps. Use a perennial ryegrass in the lawn mix as it is hard-wearing. Fine-leafed grasses don't wear well and bald patches will appear soon after the start of the cricket match.

choosing**a**playhouse

The wonderful playhouse featured in Garden 7 is secured to stout wooden supports. This creates a covered area beneath it where all the other play equipment can be stored. It also means that children have to climb a few rungs to reach the house. This adds adventure to an already exciting garden. To maintain a harmonious design the sides of the storage area are fencing panels, as used in the rest of the garden, which have

been cut to size. The front of the area is covered by a lockable door. Bright colours make the structure attractive and fun, and they also complement the planting in the rest of the garden. But what goes up must come down, especially when called in for lunch, and the plastic slide is the ideal way to get children back on terra firma, ready to eat.

Take care to scrutinize the dimensions when buying a playhouse. It has must be large enough for children to actually play in and road tests are advisable when comparing different models. The *Gardening Neighbours* playhouse is raised a metre above the ground and will not suffer from rising damp. You will need bearers or thick pieces of wood if your playhouse is to be at ground level, even if it is placed on concrete or stone slabs. These are often listed as an extra, so check the small print before buying.

Cheap cuts of rough sawn timber are often used in the manufacture of playhouses. These can result in splinters and cuts so, if your budget can stretch to it, smooth planed wood is a safer alternative. All nails, bolts and screws need to be sunk beneath the surface to prevent snagging, and all windows have to be made from shatterproof plastic.

The final decision when buying a playhouse is whether you put it up or whether the suppliers do the job. If you are brave and decide to erect the structure yourself, it is advisable to enlist a pair of helping hands. Once everything is finished, do take care entering or leaving the house. Remember that the clearance on doors is low and more and more adults are suffering from cuts and bruises as more and more children enjoy their gardens.

gardens**to**learn**in**

Children accumulate knowledge at a phenomenal rate. Between the ages of one and six years a child amasses six new words every day, so at six he or she will have a vocabulary, on average, of over 13,000 words. Manual dexterity, counting, colour recognition and reading skills are all being developed at the same time. Gardens can help with all of these.

Consider any one of the plants you want to feature in your garden. It has a name, it has leaves, it may have flowers and you may be able to eat part of it. This all makes that plant a wonderful teaching and learning aid. Counting the petals, recognizing the letters on a label, remembering the name, acknowledging the colour, touching hairy leaves, learning how to pot up, plant and harvest are skills that are easily taught and learnt skills. The thrill of spotting, for the first time, seedlings peeping through the compost is one that is never forgotten. It's at this early stage that gardeners are formed.

Even at the design stage children can be learning. Designers tell everyone to plant in odd numbers to avoid blocks of plants that look unnatural. Great advice and a super way to get young gardeners counting. Success is important to maintain interest, and cress sown on kitchen paper is quick, easy and rewarding way of learning about rates of growth, as is a competition for the largest sunflower. The largest pumpkin class at a local show is fun if you have the room to grow a prizewinner in your garden. There are other equally wonderful plants that are essential in a garden designed for children.

herbs

Herbs are a great way to learn about different smells and how plants are used in the kitchen and home. They also look good growing alongside other plants in the border, in containers or in a herb bed. Most herbs need a well-drained soil and a sunny position. The heavy clay of the gardening neighbours' soil required the addition of organic matter to improve drainage by helping to break down the large clods of clay. Raised beds also help, and soil can be imported to match the requirements of the plants.

Lavender is at home in any design and is invaluable in a garden for children. Its soft aromatic leaves, the different shapes and colours of its flowers and its many uses make it a traditional favourite. Lavender also looks terrific all the year round. The main problem is choosing which one, or which two, to incorporate into your design. French lavender (*Lavandula stoechas*) grows to 50cm (20in) and has a spread of 60cm (24in). Tufts of petals peep from the purple flower bracts in summer. To add another tick to your plant-map of the world, grow *L. angustifolia* (English lavender). Growing to 1m (3ft) with a similar spread, its unmistakable long spikes of flowers and fragrant foliage fill the summer air with perfume. A few drops of lavender oil in a warm bath will also calm down an over-excited child in readiness for a full night's sleep. This alone is a good enough reason to grow the herb. Trim off dead flower heads in autumn and your plants will stay compact and packed full of bloom year after year.

Mint is a must for the herb garden, even if it has the reputation of being a bully in flower beds and borders. It does, however, have a fascinating history that children will devour. Over 2,000 years ago the Egyptians insisted on having mint in their tombs, the Bible talks of Pharisees collecting it and the Romans carried it with them as they marched around Britain. It is also the main flavour in chewing gum and toothpaste.

There are few other plants with such a diverse range of tastes. You can grow the popular peppermint (*Mentha* x *piperita*), spearmint (*M. spicata*) and lemon mint (*M.* x *piperita* f. *citrata* 'Lemon'). Then you could have a go with ginger

Mint and lavender are perfect bed companions and ideal for a touchy feely children's garden.

mint (*M.* × *gracilis*), basil mint (*M. piperita* f. *citrata* 'Basil'), apple mint (*M. suaveolens*) and pineapple mint (*M. suaveolens* 'Pineapple'). There's even an eau-de-cologne mint (*M.* × *piperita* f. *citrata*) for older children interested in personal hygiene. Mint really does have it all.

If allowed to, each of the above will romp around the garden consuming every spare patch of soil. To prevent such a takeover, plant mint in pots sunk into the soil. The sides will restrict the rampant growth. A great alternative is to grow it above ground, in ornamental containers on a patio. A sunny or partially shaded site is ideal for growing healthy mint. If two different types are planted next to each other, the smell from each detracts from the other. It's far better to combine any one variety of mint with lavender or rosemary.

Rosemary (*Rosmarinus officinalis*) is a magical plant that's reputed to keep witches out of the garden. Another myth surrounding rosemary is that it's only supposed to thrive in gardens where the lady is the head of the house. There's a lot of it growing in the *Gardening Neighbours* gardens with mixed results. How's yours doing? For young students of history, during the plague years people stuffed rosemary into walking sticks and pockets, making full use of its power-ful fragrance to mask the smell of the dead and dying. It may be gruesome but children find this kind of fact fascinating. Rosemary will grow to 1m (3ft) with a similar spread in well-drained soil, a sunny position and out of chilling winds. The pale blue flowers in early spring kick off a perfume-packed herb year.

vegetables

Fresh vegetables are easy and fun to grow and provide children with a wealth of gardening experience and healthy eating. Children are never too young to experience the sense of

achievement that comes from growing your own produce. Eating the results is the icing on the cake.

Potatoes offer parents and guardians a fantastic opportunity to teach gardening techniques, to show children how plants develop and ensure that their young charges are eating vegetables stuffed with vitamins. Not bad for the humble spud. What's more, nothing compares with the excitement of plunging your hands into a bag of compost in search of hidden treasure. Actually there is, and that's finding some. Follow these steps for a successful crop.

1 In April roll down the sides of a large, strong plastic sack. Pierce holes in its base for drainage and put 10cm (4in) of multipurpose compost in the sack.

2 Firm the compost with your hands and place seed potatoes, available from garden centres, nurseries and mail-order catalogues, at 15cm (6in) intervals over the compost surface.

3 Place a 10cm (4in) layer of compost on top of the seed potatoes and put the sack in a sunny position. Pour in water until it runs out of the drainage holes and wait for the green shoots to appear. This will happen within two weeks.

4 Add another 10cm (4in) layer of compost to the sack. Covering the shoots with compost encourages tuber development.

5 Continue adding compost until midsummer. Keep the sack watered, even during wet weather as the dense canopy of leaves will stop rain penetrating the compost.

6 When the leaves begin to yellow, or you need potatoes for a meal, have a rummage in the sack. The tubers may be small, they may be deep down, but everyone will have a great time finding them.

Peas are easy to grow, with guaranteed results, and you haven't lived until you've popped the pods of home-grown ones. Sow the seeds either in open ground once the danger of frost has passed, or in large containers. Only choose pots with drainage holes in their bases and fill with a multipurpose compost. Children will have great fun doing this, getting up to their armpits in compost. Containers can be placed outside and seedlings will appear in around ten days.

One of the great things about peas is that they grow quickly and need to be supported with sticks or netting. Creating a wigwam with netting is fun and can, if you're feeling adventurous, be copied on a larger scale for sweet peas, runner beans or even a tepee-style hideaway. The pods soon emerge from old blooms and are ready for eating within weeks. The pop is unmissable and the taste sensational. Be prepared to accept that very few pods will make it into the kitchen as most will be eaten al fresco.

Strawberries are tempting for most children. They are also easy to grow, take up very little space, start producing fruit in under a year from planting and look spectacular when in full production. Plants grow best in a partially shaded spot out of chilly winds. An August planting will bear fruit the following June. It's not only the strawberries that fascinate children, but the intriguing way plants produce baby plantlets on runners. Make it a child's responsibility to peg these into buried pots. After a month give the leaves of a plantlet a gentle tug. Resistance indicates that roots have formed and that the time has come to sever it from its parental runner and set it up on its own.

To ensure success from the start of your strawberry adventure choose plants that are certified virus free, and watch out for and destroy slugs using biological or chemical controls. It's important to listen out for cold-weather warnings. Cover plants that are in flower with newspaper if frost is forecast, and remove the protection during the day. Strawberries can also be grown successfully in growing bags, in specially designed strawberry pots on patios and even in hanging baskets.

safety

Simple design ideas and a bit of common sense can reduce the perils lurking in the garden to a minimum.

Security: All the *Gardening Neighbours* gardens are completely fenced or walled, making them safe for children. Ensure all gates can be locked for extra security.

Soft landings: Bark chippings, used to a depth of 10cm (4in), are perfect for cushioning falls. Be sure to choose the correct grade, as different types are manufactured for different purposes. Chippings for play areas have rounded edges to eliminate the risk of splinters and cuts. Ones used to cover soil in borders usually have untreated, sharp edges and are obviously not recommended for use in a play area. The distinction is clearly made by manufacturers on product packaging.

Chippings will need topping up every year as they tend to disappear across the lawn, over the garden fence and sometimes into the soil. It is therefore best to place a semipermeable membrane on the ground before spreading the chippings. This prevents the chippings working their way into the soil. The membrane also stops weeds and stones appearing on the surface while allowing water to pass through into the soil. It is available from all garden retailers, and is rolled out like a carpet and weighed down at the edges by soil. This was the treatment given to the area around the playhouse in Garden 7. Play mats that reduce the severity of a fall are a great alternative to bark chippings.

Walls, steps and floors: Brickwork plays a large part in many gardens but is by its nature dangerous to children. In Garden 7 the walls were designed and built at a low elbows-in-the-soil

Well lit, curving steps will reduce accidents.

level which allows children to lean on them and look at the border without fear of toppling over into the plants. When a garden is built on different levels steps are inevitable, but they become less of a danger to toddlers if they are gently curved and well lit or signposted. Decking is the main flooring in many designs and requires regular cleaning to remove algae. This reduces the possibility of slippery accidents.

Water: Ponds and water features can be netted, meshed and theoretically made out of bounds to young children. But if there is water in a garden you can guarantee that children will find it and want to explore. It is safer to wait until they have become aware of the dangers posed by water features before creating ones with any depth of water. If you have inherited a pond consider transforming it into a sandpit. If, like the gardening neighbours, you have a blank canvas to design on, avoid water features altogether if the children in your garden are not quite ready for them. Shallow streams in Gardens 3 and 4 are good way to incorporate water in a garden design without introducing any extra dangers.

Pets: Family pets adore playing on bark chippings, sandpits and lawns. Unfortunately, many also consider these to be toilet areas. Parasites occur in animal droppings and do occasionally cause devastating diseases in humans. Children are susceptible to the toxocara or roundworm parasite that can cause blindness. Clear up all animal droppings and check areas before allowing children to play in them.

Tetanus: Commonly called lockjaw, this bacterial disease occurs naturally in the soil and infects through open cuts and grazes. Vaccinations are advisable every decade for adults. For children, these start before they are seven years old when the DPT (diphtheria, pertussis or whooping cough and tetanus) vaccine is administered. Keep all jabs up to date.

do's&don'ts

✓ **do** buy tools that are specially made for children. This helps them to enjoy the garden in safety and comfort.

✓ **do** let young children hamper you when you are in a hurry. Make extra time to help and encourage them, and allow them to do what you are doing, safety permitting.

✗ **don't** restrict children to a patch where you have failed to grow anything in the past. What chance will they have? Results are important, so help guarantee success.

✓ **do** read all plant labels for information on safety. Warnings are given about specific dangers.

✗ **don't** restrict children to weeding and carrying vegetation to the compost bin. Be creative and give them a paintbrush, pots of paint, packets of seed and, occasionally, the hosepipe.

Equipment and tools: In an ideal world children would never be out of your sight when they are in the garden. In reality, the siting of play equipment usually depends on available space. And, although everything for toddlers needs to be within view of a parent or guardian, older children will actually prefer a more secluded spot to develop imaginative and independent play. Here are some guidelines to making play safe.

● Swings and slides should never be situated over concrete paths. Use chippings, play mats or the lawn as a base for these.

● Erect all equipment correctly and maintain it carefully. Regularly check and tighten nuts and bolts and ensure there are no protruding nail heads on playhouses.

● It is obvious, but avoid putting football nets in front of, or next to, windows; and always use shatterproof or safety glass in greenhouses and conservatories.

● Lock rakes, spades, secateurs and all tools in a shed or storage area away from children.

● Cover the tops of plant supports like bamboo canes with eye protectors. These can be bought at garden retailers for a few pence. Alternatively use upturned empty film canisters.

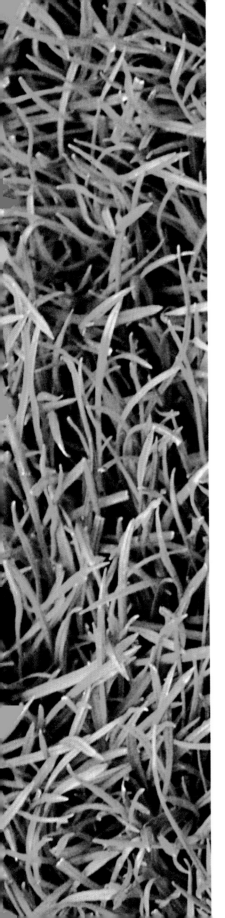

lawns

lawn *n.* a flat and usually level area of mown and cultivated grass.

for many people a garden isn't complete without a lawn, and lawns were important features in the designs for six of the eight *Gardening Neighbours* gardens. Gardeners have different uses for them, and Ali and Chris incorporated the thoughts of the gardening neighbours into their innovative creations. The lawn in Garden 7 has to withstand the constant rough and tumble of children and their friends, the one in Garden 8 will be cosseted by a devout lover of the mower dedicated to producing the best-ever lawn. For another neighbour, panache was the order of the day and the wavy lawn created by Chris in Garden 3 links style to all the other wonderful attributes of lawn ownership.

A top-class lawn enables plants and features to fuse seamlessly and form a picture of garden beauty. A super sward provides a calming complementary backdrop to surrounding plants. A quality piece of green is a reliable, constant friend in the ever-changing, always-on-the-move garden scene. It provides a piece of the countryside for many town and city dwellers. Importantly, *Gardening Neighbours* has proved that design applies as much to lawns as it does to the rest of the garden.

Lawns are no longer boring green rectangles stuck in the middle of a garden, the cause of innumerable arguments on a Sunday afternoon. Far from it: the plus points of the gardening green baize far outweigh the minuses. Indeed, the perceived workload is seen by many as therapeutic and relaxing, and the sense of achievement gained from producing a bowling-green finish is the gardening zenith.

And don't for one minute think that lawns have to be over-manicured, or tamed within a couple of centimetres of their roots. They can be a little on the wild side and still look terrific. And, in a clear case of Ali and Chris rewriting the dictionary, they don't even have to be flat and level.

Lawns can be whatever you want them to be.

a**new**lawn

There are three options when you are creating a new lawn.

grass**seed**

This is the cheapest option if you don't mind waiting for the grass to appear. After the delicate green sheen first arrives, usually within a couple of weeks of sowing the seed, another year has to elapse before the lawn is ready for heavy machinery, children, pets and size ten boots. Seed is easy to sow and, as it doesn't deteriorate if you can't immediately get round to using it, it allows you to work in the correct weather conditions.

The best time to sow grass seed is late summer or early autumn as the seedlings will have time to put roots out into warm soil before winter. Mid-spring is a good alternative as the soil has started to warm up after winter and April showers settle seedlings in nicely for the year to come. Preparation of the soil is essential so check out the guidelines shown opposite.

The chances are that the seed you are using is a mix of different types and varieties so before you start work, shake the packet to ensure they are evenly distributed.

> **'The strength of the lawn lies in providing a fine textured lush green surface, which visually unifies the elements of the design and provides harmony in the scheme'**
> *Chris Beardshaw*

1 Sow grass seed on a still day when the soil is moist. Use string to mark out metre-wide lanes across the planned area and use a couple of canes to divide the lanes into metre squares. This will help you to sow the seed at the density indicated on the packet.

2 Weigh out the required amount of seed, usually 40g (1½oz) to cover a square metre of soil, into a plastic cup and mark the level it reaches on the side of the cup. This saves you the bother of taking the scales out into the garden every time you need to weigh more seed.

3 Pour half the seed into your hand and scatter it in one direction on to a metre square of the soil surface. Pour the remaining seed into your hand and scatter this on to the soil surface at right angles to the first direction. This results in comprehensive coverage and eliminates bald patches from the outset.

4 Once all sowing is finished, gently rake the seed into the soil surface. And be gentle – all you want to do is to cover the seed, get it in contact with the soil and hide it from the birds.

5 Water the area with a gentle mist from a hosepipe, then keep the birds away by covering it with black netting weighed down around the edges with bricks. Twiggy sticks, the result of pruning trees and shrubs, are a good alternative. Seedlings will appear in a couple of weeks.

off**the**shelf**turf**

Advertised in newspapers and available from many garden centres, off-the-shelf turf is a quick way to produce an instant lawn. The green effect is immediate, and after a couple of weeks you won't be able see the joins as your carefully laid turfs knit together to form a dense, verdant carpet. The down side is that it costs a lot more to cover bare soil with turf than it does with seed and you can't choose your mix of grasses: most off-the-shelf turf contains a lot of coarse grass

soilpreparation

There's no rushing this stage, as soil preparation is the key to the success of a lawn. Ideally you should start the process at least two months before seeding, turfing or bespoke turfing.

- If, like the gardening neighbours, you have moved into a new home, you will have to remove all the rubble, stones and discarded central-heating pipes from the lawn area. Check that the cleared soil is topsoil and not nutrient-poor, badly structured subsoil dug up when the foundations of the house were put in. If in doubt, buy in quality topsoil and mix it in with your existing soil.

- Dig out dead tree-stumps as fungi will eventually form on the roots beneath the soil, causing problems in your lawn.

- Weeds have to go, and that includes their roots. Digging and forking over the area will reveal the unwanted vegetation. And while you're down there, keep picking up stones as they can be the cause of bald patches later on in the life of your lawn. Add organic matter such as rotted horse manure to the soil, removing all weeds and roots as you go.

(above) Walk on planks of wood to prevent compacting the newly cultivated soil.

(opposite) Lawn turf rolls out like carpet.

(left) Use a cultivator, available on hire, for large areas of soil.

- Levelling is important, and using pegs and a spirit level will ensure that everything is on the straight and narrow. A slight gradient away from the house is useful for drainage, especially if your garden has heavy clay soil.

- If the soil waterlogs after rain more help for drainage may be required. For a top-quality lawn, remove a 15cm (6in) layer of topsoil and spread a 5cm (2in) layer of coarse grit, available from garden centres and builders' suppliers, on the exposed surface before replacing the topsoil.

(below) Rake, rake and rake again. All stones must be removed and soil be level before sowing or turfing.

- Break down large clods by knocking them around with the back of a rake, then put on your wellies and tread all over the soil. This will firm it, reducing the chance of hollows later on, and shows where you need to add more topsoil to keep things level.

- Rake over the surface, removing annoying stones that appear from nowhere overnight, and rake again.

- Then leave everything alone. The soil will naturally settle, weed seeds will germinate and more stones will appear. Remove all the weeds and stones and rake again. You can keep doing this every week for a year, or watch out for and remove weeds every week for a month. It depends on how obsessed you are becoming with the great British lawn institution. After all, the stones will be handy for other projects in the garden such as top-dressing containers and pots.

- Check the soil level by dragging a plank over the surface and looking for hollows or excesses, then rake one last time.

- There – ready for seed or turf.

with a generous helping of weeds. You may be buying in trouble. Go to a reputable supplier, preferably one recommended by a gardening friend. However, making a turf lawn is easy, you have instant results and no problems from the peckish bird population or seeds that don't germinate. Autumn or early winter is the best time for laying turf. If you don't fancy the cold, then wait for March or April.

Ask to see and handle a sample of turf before buying. Look out for, and reject, anything with wide coarse grasses and obvious weeds. Don't buy turf with bald patches and favour turf that has been recently cut. You can see more of what you are buying if the grasses are short. Lift a length of turf, usually a metre long (around a yard) and 30 cm (12in) wide, by one end and give it a shake. It should stay intact, should not break up and should not end up in pieces at your feet. If it does, reject the whole lot and try another source.

Once you have bought quality turf it needs to be laid within a day or two. Check the weather forecast before delivery is arranged. Laying turf is a dirty job at the best of times, but a nightmare when it's wet. Choose a day when no rain is due and the soil isn't too moist. Stack the turf in rolls when it's delivered to prevent drying out. If you can't lay it for a couple of days open the rolls out in a shady spot and keep them watered until you or your soil are ready. Preparation of the soil is essential, so check out the guidelines on the previous page.

1 Lay a row of single length of turf on your prepared soil ensuring that each one is pressed closely against the next. Gently tamp each turf down and check the level with a board and spirit level. Remove or add soil beneath a turf to achieve a flat surface. Never beat it into submission to make it fit.

2 Now lay a second row to form a stretcher bond effect. Imagine you are making a horizontal wall of grass and everything will work out. Again press turfs closely together to ensure a fantastic finish. Keep plenty of planks handy as

Kneel on planks to avoid damaging newly laid turfs. Butt edges together to form a horizontal lawn wall.

walking on newly laid turf will cause damage. Avoid using a small piece of turf to finish off a row as it will invariably lift, shift and cause problems. As you get towards the end of a row it is better to lay a full length from the end inwards and use the smaller piece to fill in the resultant gap. Another method is to deliberately overrun your proposed edge by 10cm (4in) and cut the excess off with a knife once the turf is established.

3 Keep going until the area is covered and you are nearly the owner of a newly laid lawn.

4 Walk on the planks and brush a mixture of equal parts loam, peat and sand into all the cracks and joins between the turfs to help the edges knit together and the turf to establish. Loam-based seed compost is an easily bought ready-made alternative.

5 Keep the lawn well watered in dry weather, using a hosepipe and sprinkler if the water authorities allow.

6 Allow the turf to establish and put roots down for a couple of months, then shape the edges to fit your design. Straight lines are easy to cut with a half-moon edging iron. Indicate the line of a meandering edge by placing a hosepipe on the surface of the lawn. If possible, check the shape from an upstairs room to ensure that the edge is pleasing. Even better, get a friend to guide you from the window. Sand poured from a plastic soft-drinks bottle is also a good way to mark out an edge before making the first cut.

seedtypes

Do you want a great-looking lawn that has to endure the odd football match and a marauding dog or two? If yes, look for a grass seed mix containing perennial ryegrass.

Do you want one that has a surface like the top of a snooker table and doesn't have to withstand heavy wear and tear? If yes, look for a grass seed mix without perennial ryegrass.

Perennial ryegrass traditionally has a broad, coarse leaf and doesn't look as fine as other types, but is more resilient and hardwearing. Its seeds are also the cheapest ones to put in a mix. However, there is now a perennial ryegrass which has fine leaves and which is therefore hard-wearing and great looking. Suppliers of grass seed know this is a good thing and shout about it on their packaging. It's worth checking this type out at your local supplier.

Mixtures of grass seed for specific soil types and conditions – clay soil, sandy soil and shady areas – are all readily available. Match the seed mixture to your conditions and requirements.

Check the type of seed used in any turf you buy. Children play all over Garden 7 and a turf containing perennial ryegrass was chosen. After a couple of false starts, the mower-lover dedicated to his lawn selected a fine-leaf mix for his bespoke turf in Garden 8, with fantastic results.

bespoke**turf**

Bespoke, or seeded, turf combines the benefits of seed sowing and turf laying and was used in all the *Gardening Neighbours* gardens. You know the mix of grasses and it's easy to lay, with instant results. Of course, it costs more than ordinary turf or seed but if you want a top-quality lawn within hours look for suppliers of bespoke turf. At the turf farm the seed is sown through a fine mesh onto a specially formulated soil mixture. It germinates and grows, and the turfs are cut and lifted to order by special turf-lifting machines. All you have to do is buy the finished product and follow the previously described turf-laying procedure. The fine mesh binds the roots together, making each length easy to lay. It's worth asking the supplier for a small bag of the actual seed used in the mix. This can be combined with the loam, sand and peat when you fill in the joins between turfs.

that**lawn**explained

Chris's wavy lawn for Garden 3 is certainly at the cutting edge of design, but what about the practicalities? Does anyone make a lawnmower small enough to hover over the peaks and yet dip into the troughs, avoiding scalping and missing? What happened to the definition of a lawn as a flat area? Is all the information about removing humps and lumps a waste of time?

Chris says that the measurement of the distance between ridge and trough and the height reduction allows a small hover mower to cut it effectively. 'This was all taken into account at the design stage,' he says. The great thing about design ideas is that you can give them a go and break the rules. If you fancy something, have a shot at it. Remember, though, that even when producing a creation as stunning as the wavy lawn the same amount of detail needs to be applied to soil preparation and seed or turf choice. The heavy clay soil in Garden 3 allowed the mounds beneath the turf to be easily moulded. To create the waves the length of the lawn was measured and the point between each of the peaks was measured and replicated along the total lawn length. A stunning and workable design.

(left) Firm soil to avoid slippage later when hollows are harder to repair.

(below) Even on wavy lawns, roll out turf firmly on to the soil.

(below) Low voltage lights in each of the troughs creates a stunning lawn.

grassalternatives

If the thought of a tightly manicured lawn conjures up too much tradition and work, there are alternatives that look equally impressive in most gardens.

meadow**lawn**

A meadow is a patch of land covered in grass – usually broad-leafed ryegrass varieties – in which weeds grow and flourish, and looks best in larger gardens where it's left to its own devices. Soil preparation is important when planning a meadow lawn. Remove all stones as you would for a bowling-green lawn and sow a specially mixed seed or lay meadow turf. Depending on the overall effect you want, mowing can start when seedlings reach 8cm (3in) tall or you can forget about it for three months. Once established a meadow lawn only needs mowing, using a line trimmer, twice a year. The final cut of the year takes place in September.

If you or your designer feel that your garden isn't large enough for a full-scale lawn like this, pathways or areas beneath trees also look wonderfully wild when converted to meadow.

wild-flower**meadow**

A wild-flower meadow is similar to a meadow but the flowers are sown by the owner. Although you have some control over what you are producing it does look untamed, so think carefully about converting all your lawn space. However, smaller patches or drifts blend beautifully into most garden designs. Alternatively, pathways can be mown to give more structure to the wild look of the meadow. For a successful wild-flower lawn to develop you need nutrient-poor soil. The last thing wild flowers need is fertilizer. Nature doesn't give it to them, so don't be tempted to treat them to a handful of balanced fertilizer as you will only encourage taller grasses at the expense of the flowers.

Mixed seeds are available – just scatter them on the soil and rake them in – and wild flowers are also packaged individually, allowing the gardener to select his or her favourites. The choice is gratifyingly extensive, but try growing the following from seed if you want months of floriferous frenzy.

Common dog violet (*Viola riviniana*) is a beautiful plant that grows in clumps to 15cm (6in) high. The mauve flowers are produced in April. Enjoys the semi-shaded conditions of a wild-flower meadow.

Cuckoo flower (*Cardamine pratensis*) is a tall plant that grow to 45cm (18in) high with small lilac-coloured flowers in May. Provide a damp area and watch this beauty flourish.

Lesser celandine (*Ranunculus ficaria*) is a rampant, mat-forming plant that grows to 10cm (4in) high and will gladly romp around your wild-flower meadow. The small heart-shaped leaves smother the soil surface while buttercup-yellow flowers wave cheerfully from tall spikes in June.

Wild marjoram (*Origanum vulgare*) is a gorgeous woody plant that grows to 45cm (18in) high and has dark green, oval aromatic leaves. Tubular mauve flowers are produced on top of wiry stems in July.

Harebell (*Campanula rotundifolia*) is a favourite wild flower for chalky soil where it grows to 25cm (10in) high. Pendant azure-blue blooms are produced on thin flower stalks in August.

The knapweed family (*Centaurea* species) consists of lots of different varieties all of which enjoy a drier position in the wild-flower meadow. Thistle-like flowers, in various shades of blue, red and white, are produced in September on plants 60cm (24in) high.

A bench placed behind a camomile lawn creates a restful spot in Garden 6.

Common toadflax (*Linaria vulgaris*) has grey-green leaves that, alone, are worth the price of the packet of seed, with the bonus of wallflower-like blooms in strong yellow making this a must-grow plant. Growing to 60cm (24in) and flowering in October, it fills that early autumn flower gap and will give your wildflower meadow a welcome boost.

Chamomile (*Chamaemelum nobile*) was fashionable for lawns before the tight-cropped bowling greens favoured by many people today became a gardening obsession. If you fancy growing a chamomile lawn look out for *C. nobile* 'Treneague'. It doesn't produce flowers, but when walked upon it gives off a wonderful fruity aroma. It is short-growing and therefore ideal as a lawn. Only attempt one of these lawns in a sunny site and on well-drained soil. In Garden 6 a chamomile mini-lawn is perfectly situated in

front of the owner's favourite garden bench. On every visit she enjoys the fragrance and appearance of this evergreen mat-forming plant. The lawn was raised up so drainage is perfect, even in an area of heavy clay soil.

Before planting, clear the soil of stones and weeds. Ensure it is level by treading over the surface, raking and levelling. Individual plants can be bought from garden centres and nurseries. Each one should be planted 15cm (6in) apart in all directions. The lawn will look sparse at first, but the plants will soon grow to meet their neighbours and form a dense carpet of aromatic leaves. Each plant will grow to 10cm (4in) high and the lawn can be either mowed with the mower blades set high or, in smaller areas, cut with garden shears. To help plants develop quickly, keep them watered in dry spells. Bare patches will occur – they always do – so keep a small supply of plants growing in pots as quick-fix substitutes.

Creeping thymes are fantastic as lawns, and a real pleasure to plant. The hardest part is choosing a variety as there are so many on offer. Wild creeping thyme (*Thymus polytrichus* subsp. *britannicus*) grows to 3cm (just over 1in) high, spreads 20cm (8in) and sports pale mauve flowers in summer. *T. serpyllum coccineus* 'Major' grows to a similar size and has red flowers. For pink flowers try *T. serpyllum* 'Annie Hall'. If white flowers are your thing go for *T. serpyllum* 'Lemon Curd', a gorgeous plant that produces white flowers tinged with pink throughout summer, above bright green lemon-scented leaves. Considering that all the creeping thymes grow to approximately the same height, a mix of the named varieties would look amazing. The kaleidoscope of flower colour combined with the patchwork of fragrant foliage could be the highlight of many gardens.

Thymes grow all over the world but many originate in the warm, dry conditions of the Mediterranean. This gives gardeners a clue to their likes and dislikes. Well-drained soil in a sunny position is preferable to cold, damp waterlogged conditions.

Plant individuals 15cm (6in) apart in all directions and keep watered in dry spells when young. Again, keep a few spares growing in pots for repairs.

bulbs**for**added**value**

Planting bulbs that flower in spring is a traditional way to add even more interest to lawns. Planting is done in autumn and is easy. Use a spade to cut away flaps of established turf to expose the soil. Then you have a choice, and what you choose may be determined by your personality. If you want order in your garden, arrange your chosen bulbs in straight, military rows on the exposed soil, replace the turf and pat everything into place. If you want a more anarchic look, drop the bulbs on the soil, stand them

the correct way up and replace the grass; or turn your back on your lawn, throw a handful of bulbs over your shoulder, turn round and get planting. Using a bulb planter removes the need for any spadework.

The theory is that bulbs push their way up through the grass, flower, replenish food reserves through their leaves and die down ready for next year. And theory is turned into reality provided you allow the bulb shoots to grow in spring and the leaves to die down naturally in summer before getting the mower out. This makes planting bulbs perfect for meadow lawns and wild-flower meadows, but a little tricky in the bowling-green lawn. And then there are the summer-flowering bulbs that are planted in spring. The same rules about waiting for their leaves to die down apply, so think carefully about where you are going to naturalize bulbs if you are a pro-lawner proud of the green-baize look. Don't forget that bulbs are effective under trees where they can be left alone to do their own thing while you are busy mowing, trimming and edging.

The choice of bulbs, as in most aspects of gardening, is staggering but the following are guaranteed winners.

Daffodils (*Narcissi*) require no introduction or description as the humble daff nestles securely in the nation's gardening hearts. There are so many different varieties to choose from that is almost impossible to suggest just one, but *Narcissus* 'Spellbinder' has to be seen to be believed. The gorgeous yellow trumpets on flower stalks 30cm (12in) high are produced in March and fade to white over a couple of weeks. Plant the bulbs 15cm (6in) deep in September for blooms the following March.

Star of Bethlehem (*Ornithogalum umbellatum*) is a white, star-shaped flower that gazes up at you from a height of 30cm (12in). Each bulb, planted 5cm (2in) deep in October, will produce a clump of strappy green leaves followed by blooms in

extras**for**individuality

Brushing your lawn to create different patterns is a wonderful way to create an individual look. It is ideally suited to larger lawns, but still applicable to smaller versions. All you need is a morning when heavy dew has descended and a stiff brush. At the crack of dawn venture into the garden with your brush and sweep patterns onto the surface of the lawn. Be careful always to place your feet on a part that has been swept as footprints may ruin the effect. The pattern will only last a few hours – as the temperature rises, the dew and your handiwork will disappear forever.

Weeds can add interest at no cost. In fact, not treating a lawn and allowing them to grow will save money and time. A lawn overrun by weeds may look untidy, but the controlled speckling supplied by a crop of daisies can look charming, evoking memories of warm summer days in the countryside. Even a small patch of daisy-dotted lawn is delightful.

June. This beauty isn't fussy about conditions, growing equally well in shade or sun, and is perfect for naturalizing on well-drained soil. It must be one of the few stars that actually disappears at night. As darkness falls the flowers close into a restful sleep, tired after the exertions of attracting the summer bees.

Wake robin, wood lily (*Trillium grandiflorum*) is a woodland plant. Getting it going can be a little tricky, but has to be worth all the effort. The 5cm (2in) wide flowers turn from pearl-white to pink in May if rhizomes are planted 8cm (3in) deep in August. The trick is to provide shade for the leaves and plenty of organic matter like well-rotted horse manure for the roots. Once planted, leave it alone to form clumps that can, after a few years growth, be lifted, divided and immediately replanted. Simple flowers with three petals are its trademark.

Erythronium **'Pagoda'** has beautiful yellow flowers that are produced in April if the corms are planted 8cm (3in) deep in September. Ideally at home in a woodland setting, the corms are perfect for the meadow situation, naturalizing in long grass. The plants, 25cm (10in) tall, produce their blooms on wiry stems. Partial shade is best

and moisture-retentive soil a must. When buying the corms at a garden centre ensure they are still moist. If they are allowed to dry out they won't grow. It goes without saying that you need to plant them once you get home and in the garden.

Quamash (*Camassia cusickii*) is becoming a trendsetter. It may the stunning azure-blue flowers. It may be sheer flower power with up to a hundred blooms per spike. It may be the fact that the bulbs will thrive in heavy, wet soil such as that encountered in the *Gardening Neighbours* gardens. But who cares why – it just needs to be grown in every possible naturalizing position. Plant the bulbs 10cm (4in) deep during September and wait for the flower spikes to appear the following June. The blues will chase away the dark clouds of a British summer.

Spring starflower (*Ipheion uniflorum*) is an enchanting washed-blue flower with a delightfully simple name. Plant the bulbs 5cm (2in) deep in September and blooms will be produced on stalks the following April. The plants grow to 15cm (6in) high and have thick, strappy leaves that give off a pungent garlic smell when crushed. So, depending on your taste, plant near to, or far away from, a walkway in your meadow lawn. Spring starflowers have no particular soil requirements, but keep them out of a windy position for best results.

Mouse plant (*Arisarum proboscideum*) has a curious flower that produces a long tail resembling the back end of a mouse disappearing through a gnawed piece of skirting board. The base of the flower is white, the top is purplish-brown and the mouse's tail is a definite purple. The plants grow to around 10cm (4in) high with a similar spread and produce arrow-shaped leaves. The blooms themselves are tiny, but the tails can trail for 15cm (6in). Plant the tubers 15cm (6in) deep during September and keep a close eye out for flowers in March.

mowing

Newly seeded lawns can have their first cut when the grass is 5cm (2in) high. Ideally this should be done with sharp garden shears as this avoids the young roots being disturbed by heavy mowers. If the area is too big for you to contemplate the use of shears – and all the lawned areas in the *Gardening Neighbours* gardens are at the limit of being shear-friendly – use a hover-type mower with the blades set as high as possible. Pick a day when the grass is dry to prevent any tearing by the blades. Allow the grass to regrow to 5cm (2in) and then start cutting regularly with the blades set to leave 3cm (just over an inch) of grass.

Newly turfed lawns can have their first cut a month after laying. Roots will have ventured into the soil and the turfs will be able to withstand machinery. Be watchful for any joins between individual turfs that may have lifted slightly as these will snag in your machine and the grass will be damaged.

It is always best to check over new and established lawns before mowing. Remove stones or twigs that may cause damage to mower blades. Brush damp grass to remove dew (creating patterns if the fancy takes you) as this makes mowing more efficient, reduces clogging of the cutting blades and most of the grass will stand up, ready to be cut.

Mower blades must be sharp for a fine cut. Have replacement blades or sharpening tools handy.

buying**mowers**

There are many types of mower and the amount of money you are prepared to spend usually dictates the machine you buy. The following points are worth thinking about before purchasing this expensive gardening item.

Power supplies:

Hand push – Perfect for that traditional sound, and superb quality of cut. Tiring when tackling a large lawn, great for all the *Gardening Neighbours*, but check the weight of the mower with a trial run before buying.

Electric – Lightweight, inexpensive and best for a medium-sized lawn. Check the length of flex and availability of a power supply. Spare parts freely available from most garden retailers.

Petrol – Noisy and expensive, but powerful. Doesn't require trailing leads or an external power source. Great for large lawns.

Style of cutting:

Cylinder action – Blades rotate and cut the grass against a static base-blade. The greater the number of blades and the faster the rotation, the better the quality of cut.

Rotary action – A blade rotates horizontally at high speed beneath the mower body which is is held up either by wheels or an air cushion. The former is called a rotary wheeled mower, the latter a hover mower.

Line trimmer – A plastic cord rotates at high speeds and slices through the grass – an asset to the lawn in Garden 3.

safe**mowing**

✓ **only** cut grass when it is dry.

✗ **don't** mow in the rain.

✓ **always** wear gardening boots or strong shoes.

✗ **never** look under a mower until the blade has stopped and the power supply has been turned off.

✓ **always** switch the mower off before adjusting a blade.

✗ **never** clean a machine when the power supply on.

✓ **always** use a residual current device (RCD) with an electric mower. This stops the current if you slice through the flex or if some other electrical problem occurs. It may save your life. Available from all electrical retailers, the RCD plugs into a wall socket and your electric mower plugs into the device.

Accessories:

Rollers – Essential for that stripy lawn effect.

Grass box – Always use one to collect the clippings.

Other points to watch out for:

- Look at the braking systems of different models to see how quickly the blade stops when the power supply is switched off.
- Check whether the mower will fold away or hang vertically. This saves shed space and grazed knees and elbows. Buying a larger shed is not usually a viable option.
- Check on the availability of spares, especially cutting blades and lines.
- Determine how easy it is to adjust the height of the cutting blades. Fiddly adjustments might stop you performing a vital part of the mowing regime. Ask the sales assistant to show you how to adjust the blades.

worn-out**lawns**

The gardening neighbours were lucky in that they had nothing in their gardens when they started. It is often easier to begin a project from scratch than try to turn old, worn-out features into something worth keeping. However, many gardeners do just that and tired lawns are usually the first assignment that needs tackling.

Mowing is essential if a top-grade lawn is to be achieved and a clean cut will reveal the true condition of your lawn. Chances are that weeds and moss have become dominant at the expense of the grass. Treating a lawn with the appropriate chemical weedkillers is an effective way to contain and control the problem – but getting it fit to fight weed attacks is the best solution.

Raking or scarifying opens up the surface of compacted soil, allowing air to enter and healthy grass roots to develop. If the soil is solid and your rake merely scratches at the surface of the problem, spike all over the area with a garden fork. Insert the tines to a depth of 10cm (4in) and waggle the handle forwards and backwards to create holes. Brush a mix of peat, sand and loam into the holes, as you would when turfing. Incorporate grass seed in the mix to get your rejuvenation programme off to a flying start. Bare patches are inevitable once weeds and moss have gone, so you will have to reseed or returf the lawn. Special seed mixes for patching give quick results.

Broken and tatty edges are a common problem with tired lawns. Cutting a piece of the offending turf, lifting and turning it so that the broken edge is inside the lawn easily rectifies this eyesore. The repositioned broken edge can be reseeded or returfed in the usual way. It's a quick way to perk up an edge.

If one particular area is worn out because of heavy foot traffic, a redesign is required. Very often a lawn is accessed at one point, and one point only. Simply moving a pot, removing part of a wall or replanting a flower bed can open up alternative routes.

Once the corrective treatment has been carried out, stick to a regular mowing regime, control weeds as appropriate and feed the lawn.

Butt edges together and fill all cracks and joins with compost and, if possible, a matching seed mix.

what**next**?

Meadow, wildflower, chamomile and thyme lawns all look after themselves, give or take a bit of patching, planting and the occasional mowing. The traditional bowling-green lawn loved by many, but not all, of the gardening neighbours involves more work but is readily achievable.

- Regular mowing is essential, with 'little and often' being the maxim for a top-class lawn. Many experts advise leaving clippings on the lawn. They claim the nutrients are fed back into the soil. However, the build-up of dead grass, called thatch, can suffocate the live grass, so collect and compost the clippings every time you mow. A lawn also looks much better when it's clear of debris. The only time clippings aren't put on the compost heap is when weedkillers have been used on the lawn. Allow six months to elapse between the final weedkiller treatment and composting clippings.

- Keep all lawn edges under control by trimming every time you mow. If the trimmings fall onto soil they should be hoed into the top layer. A line of bricks, wood, metal or plastic can be used as a mowing strip. Sink it slightly lower than the level of the lawn to allow the mower to fizz over it, cleanly cutting every

Garden 6 has a magnificent lawned area with a focal point that takes the eye around the gorgeous features in the borders.

monthly**checklist**

January Avoid walking on frozen grass. Check over and service the mower.

February Begin soil preparation for seeding. Source and buy seed requirements.

March Rake, mow and edge. Watch out for, and eliminate, moss and weeds.

April Plant summer-flowering bulbs for naturalizing in established meadow and wildflower lawns or under trees. Continue regular mowing and edging. Sow lawn seed in prepared soil.

May Sow lawn seed in prepared soil. Continue mowing and edging. Feed with a nitrogen-rich fertilizer. Aerate and top-dress with a sand, peat and loam mix.

June Mow, edge, feed. Watch for weeds and treat if necessary. Water if the lawn is dry.

July Mow, edge, feed.

August Mow, edge.

September Switch to autumn lawn fertilizer. Sow seed. Plant naturalizing spring-flowering bulbs in meadow and wildflower lawns and under trees.

October Regular mowing is finished for the year. Sweep up leaves and lay turf. Plant more spring-flowering bulbs for naturalizing.

November Lay turf in non-frosty conditions. Sweep up leaves. Clean and oil mowers.

December Redesign, if necessary, the lawn.

blade of grass. The owner of Garden 8 uses a thin strip of wood notched through half of its thickness at regular intervals. The notches allow the wood to follow the line of the lawn, providing a mowing strip and a demarcation between the lawn and flower beds. Brick edges were used in most of the other gardens to great effect.

- Feeding a lawn is important to encourage deep colour and strong growth. In spring and summer a fertilizer high in nitrogen is required. This encourages lush, green growth and more mowing, but it does lead to a top-class bowling-green finish. Check the levels of nitrogen on manufacturers' packaging.

- Feed the lawn with a balanced fertilizer in autumn. This helps a healthy root system to develop and strong leaf growth to appear the following spring. Specially formulated autumn lawn food is available. Never use a fertilizer high in nitrogen in autumn as the resultant soft growth is easily damaged by winter weather.

- Rake the lawn once a month to aerate the soil and remove all debris.

- Treat any unwanted weeds immediately they pop up and before they flower. You can use chemicals but a small hand fork is sometimes better. Make sure all deep roots are removed to prevent regrowth.

- Investigate the cause of moss infestations – usually poor drainage. Treat the cause and kill the moss.

- Worms occasionally ruin the appearance of a lawn by leaving soil casts on the surface. Brush these over the entire lawn before mowing. If left, they will provide a seedbed for weeds.

- Remove fallen leaves from the lawn in autumn.

- Aerate the lawn twice a year and top-dress it with a loam, sand and peat mix.

- Choose the correct mower for your lawn and keep it clean and serviced.

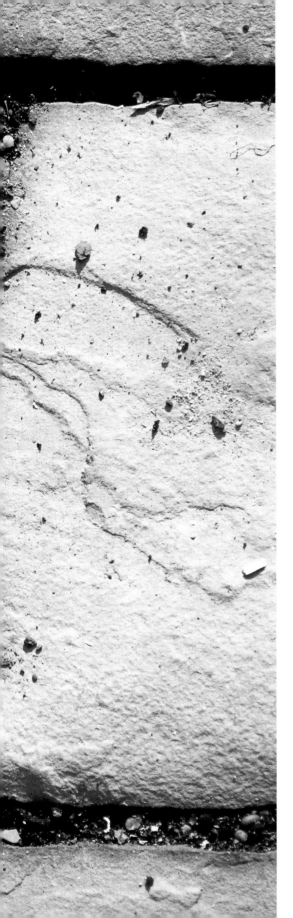

chapter**eight**

problem
areas

problem *n.* any thing, matter, person, etc., that is
difficult to deal with.

the old adage that there are no problems, merely
opportunities, is fitting in a garden situation. The
gardening neighbours had plenty of opportunities for
creative gardening when confronted by their bare
pieces of earth. The first was to deal with the soil – the
starting point for anyone taking over a garden. Get it
right and the rest will follow. With the assistance of
tons of organic matter the heavy clay soil in their
gardens was persuaded to behave, and design plans
were put into action.

Only when the soil has been dealt with do other
opportunities arise, such as the chance to find solutions for a dark area that gets no water, areas of
extreme sun and a host of other challenges. These are
numerous and vary from garden to garden. Simple
features like drains cause endless headaches but are
easily rectified. Next door's caravan or barking dogs
do present more of a challenge. With Chris and Ali's
expert design and gardening skills, the gardening
neighbours solved the problems and really did see
them as opportunities.

dealing**with**soil

Heavy clay and pure sand both give gardeners opportunities to grow specific plants. One option, therefore, is to live and garden with your soil and change nothing; merely match plants and features to the prevalent conditions. Plants suited to particular soil types are detailed on page 86. The alternative is to plough in tons of organic matter, as the gardening neighbours did, to allow a wider choice of plants to be grown.

If you take over an established garden water-logged soil may not reveal itself for months, possibly after plants have been planted and features placed. What was beautiful garden soil in a dry spring may turn into a muddy morass in winter, killing the plants and floating the features. The options are to check the year-round conditions in your garden by waiting until twelve months have elapsed before tackling anything, or checking the drainage.

- At the lowest part of your garden, dig a hole 60cm (2ft) square and 90cm (36in) deep.
- Wait for a spell of wet weather, put your wellies on and check the hole.
- If there is no water in the hole an hour after the rain has stopped the drainage is excessively efficient. You probably have sandy soil and your work will be cut out adding tons of organic matter to help it retain water and prevent plants wilting in hot weather.
- If the water drains out of the hole within two days of the rain stopping, your drainage is perfect.
- If 5cm (2in) of water is present two days after the rain has stopped, improve the drainage by digging in organic matter or grit. Only do this when the soil is dry.
- If the hole is half full a few days after the rain has stopped, extra drainage is required.

Drainage systems are expensive so it is wise to find out why the soil is waterlogging before spending money and time on tile drains or soak-

aways. A high water-table will cause water-logging on clay soil. There is nothing you can do about lowering this layer of saturated, porous rock, but you can import soil and raise the level of your garden. If clay isn't the reason for reduced drainage there may be a solid layer or pan of soil under the topsoil. Dig around and check the condition of your subsoil. If it is non-porous, it's a case of raised beds or moving house.

Whatever the reason for your problem, once you're satisfied that you want to spend money on a drainage system, you have a choice between tile drains and soakaways. Both are laid 30cm (12in) beneath the surface and consist of a 2m (6ft) layer of broken bricks or stones. The only difference between them is that tile drains have a network of pipes that carry the water away to another water-course, whereas soakaways do not. Always check with drainage experts and your local authority before installing a drainage system.

access**points**

It's all very well decking out walkways and smothering areas with turf, but you or future workpeople will need access to drains, meters and grids. Inspection-chamber covers are not the prettiest things in the world, but are easily disguised. A container of alpines looks terrific all year round and can be moved away when the drains need inspecting. Slightly raise it off the ground to help drainage and make it easier to lift.

Another solution are plants with long trailing stems which can be grown nearby. The stems will trail over the cover and are easily moved aside when access is required. A beautiful plant ideal for this purpose would be one of the Californian lilacs (*Ceanothus thyrsiflorus* var. *repens*). Leaves are present all year round on mound-shaped plants that spread 2.5m (8ft). Plant it away from the manhole cover and allow its branches to grow and do their covering act. All *Ceanothus* plants need a sunny position in well-drained soil. Periwinkles (*Vinca* species), with their trailing stems adorned with blue flowers, are perfect for long-distance covering. But beware: they can take over a border and enjoy sun or shade, wet or dry soil.

In Garden 1, where wooden decking covered an inspection chamber, a removable access point (shown here) was cut into the boards to enable access to the drains. It looks like an integral part of the decking and is easily made. Tie a piece of string to a nail or screw driven into the decking above the centre of the service hatch. Tie a pencil to the other end and draw a perfect circle on the boards. Remove the nail and screw. Use a jigsaw to cut the circle.

weeds**and**weeding

Whether you take over an established garden or a new plot, weeds will quickly raise their heads. They are merely plants in the wrong place at the wrong time. Many are beautiful individuals and are often useful in supplying food for caterpillars, natural pesticides and plant food. Nettles do all this and if you can bear the thought of allowing a patch to thrive, your garden will be better for it. Other weeds are blatantly aggressive and it takes a botanist to appreciate their beauty. In many cases, weeds have natures that only their mothers can love.

There are two groups of weeds: annuals and perennials.

Annual weeds do everything they need to do in one growing season. They grow, flower, set seed, disperse seed and die in one growing season. The trick is to stop their life cycle by removing all of them before they set seed. You will save hours of weeding at a later date. If you allow an annual weed to set and disperse seed you can expect to see its offspring for the next few years. Triumphantly walking down a garden with a dead weed, but one that has set seed, in your hand is only helping with seed dispersal. Fat hen (*Chenopodium album*) is a lovely example of an annual weed and produces delicate white flowers from the axils of large, green leaves on plants 30cm (12in) high. The seeds are quickly produced and dispersed around your garden, with resultant seedlings popping up all over the place.

Perennial weeds grow year after year, and usually spread further afield by underground runners or roots. They survive the winter by storing food beneath the soil in storage organs, and spring into life when the soil warms up. Their food reserves need to be cut off, and this is done by removing the leaves, their food factory. Field horsetail, mare's tail or horsetail (*Equisetum arvense*) are common names for the same ancient, perennial weed. The shoots resemble miniature Christmas trees and if potted in a terracotta pot will look fantastic. The underground network of roots spreads throughout the garden, sending up feathery shoots everywhere. They can crack concrete paths, push brickwork to one side and cause real problems when they grow up through decking slats. If you dig down and slice through a root, a shoot will form at the cut – so don't.

dealing**with**weeds

Pulling weeds out by hand will remove many annual ones and reduce the vigour of perennials. It's a great way to remove small numbers of the less invasive weeds and a chance to get to know your soil and garden from close quarters.

- Hoeing weeds is kinder to your back and a good way to clear larger areas of both annuals and the top growth of perennial weeds. Keep the blade of your hoe clean and sharp, but take care when weeding around valuable shrubs. It has been known for seedlings and the shoots of bulbs to be hoed off by enthusiastic gardeners. Label the places where bulbs have been planted.
- Placing a layer of material on the soil suppresses weeds. Organic mulches, such as

do's**&**don'ts

✓ **do** keep weedkillers in sealed containers away from young hands.

✗ **don't** use them near wildlife areas.

✓ **do** wear gloves and eye protectors when applying weedkillers as many of them can cause skin irritations.

✗ **don't** use weedkillers on windy days as drifting spray may damage desirable plants.

✓ **do** make sure the product you use is suitable for the weeds you are tackling.

✗ **don't** use a watering can usually reserved for feeding as contamination is inevitable.

✓ **do** read all packaging carefully and use as recommended.

Dig out stones and builder's rubble. Dig in organic matter to get the soil in shape for plants.

bark chippings, keep them down and retain water. Any weeds that do grow in the loose chippings are easily pulled out.

Pebbles were used to cover the entire surface area in Garden 4. As pebbles alone do not suppress weeds, weeding such an area would be time-consuming. Ali first covered the soil with a planting membrane. This woven material allows water to pass down through to the soil, but nothing to grow up. It is easily cut to allow plants to be planted in the soil. Flaps of the membrane are folded back around the base of stems to ensure coverage of the soil. After planting, the pebbles were poured over the surface. The only weeds that will attempt to grow will be from airborne seeds which will never take hold in the layer of pebbles.

● Digging over virgin soil will reveal many perennial roots which should be removed and burnt. Don't add them to the compost heap as the temperatures it generates may not be high enough to kill roots and the subsequent compost will carry the weeds. Turning the top spade-depth of soil over will bury many annual seeds too deep for them to grow. However, other more deep-lying ones will be exposed and may start to germinate. This often happens with poppy seeds after a field has been ploughed.

● Chemicals are often called into action when tackling weeds. Herbicides can either be selective, killing one particular plant and nothing else, or non-selective, killing anything green. Each type can then be divided into ones that are applied to foliage or to the soil.

Foliage-applied herbicides enter plants through the leaves. They either kill weeds on contact – the leaves wither within days – or move through plants killing them as they go, eventually wiping out their root systems. Herbicides applied to the soil enter plants through the roots. They can stay active for weeks, killing any weed seed that dares to germinate below the surface of the soil. All weedkillers are, of course, chemicals and therefore have no place in organic gardens.

Weeds can provide an opportunity to grow gorgeous plants, and often the chance to deceive a neighbour. Try growing some of the perennial types in containers where roots will not be able to escape and invade the rest of the garden. Avoid doing this with annual ones as once they have set seed you'll be stuck with them for a few years.

sheds**and**such

Sheds, playhouses and summer houses can dominate a garden. There are two schools of thought: either keep the structure quiet or allow it to shout out loud. The gardening neighbours did both. In Garden 1 the shed housed the family dog and as both dog and shed were large the shed was always going to dominate the garden. Chris positioned it so that the longest wall runs away from the eye, rather than across the line of vision. From the house, it instantly appeared smaller. It was painted the same dark blue as the boundary fences, further adding to the camouflage. Finally the shed and immediate area were fenced off to prevent the dog marauding around the plot. Solid fencing would have resulted in a visual shortening of the garden, but open lattice-style panels don't add to the problem. Rather, they create an opportunity to grow fantastic climbing plants. Paving the area around the shed keeps muddy paw marks off the fantastic decking in the rest of the garden.

> **'Make them an integral part of the scheme using the same design effort as in other areas of the garden; just because it performs a utility function does not automatically mean it has to be a utilitarian design'**
> *Chris Beardshaw on hiding an ugly compost bin*

Ali adopted the opposite tactic in positioning and painting the children's playhouse in Garden 7. Ali wanted the structure to be highly visible, fun and colourful. Placing it in a corner gave it protection from the elements without intruding too much on the garden. Positioning the playhouse so that its door faces the house is important to allow careful parental surveillance. The colours are bold without being dominant and raising the structure on supports makes full use of the vertical free space while creating a storage area beneath. The structure has become an integral part of the garden.

The summer house in Garden 2 was placed in a dominant position because of its inherent beauty. Not only does it look great from all

dealing**with**light

Hot, baking sun will frazzle certain plants within days. Likewise, the dark depths of a shaded corner will cause sun-lovers to stretch, pale and suffer. Match the plants, just as Chris and Ali did in the *Gardening Neighbours* gardens, to their ideal conditions, as detailed in Chapter 4.

However, some plants can play a part in producing ideal conditions for others in problem areas. Position a tree in a sun-drenched site to cast gentle, dappled shade, and grow a host of plants beneath it. It will also be a great place for a bench or seating. Shaded areas are shaded for a reason. Overhanging branches or hedges are often responsible and should be sawn off or trimmed. If they belong to a neighbouring garden it is vital to ask permission before getting the pruning saw or loppers out.

(opposite) Lattice style fencing takes the emphasis off the shed, yet allows an open feel to Garden 1.

(below) Painted matching colours, the shed is hardly noticeable.

angles, the garden looks great when viewed from inside the summer house.

Greenhouses feature in many gardens and sometimes have to be positioned out of sight as they can look unattractive. Disguise is one option, but a well-filled greenhouse bursting with colour is awesome. Ideally, it should be away from overhanging trees that will cast shade. If you'll be using electricity, place the greenhouse near an outdoor socket or close to the house to allow economical cable-laying. If your design allows, run the largest wall of the structure on an east–west axis. This will ensure that you make full use of the sun and won't cast self-shadows within the structure.

Before erecting any structure in the garden check with the local authorities to ensure planning permission isn't required and, as a matter of courtesy, discuss it with your neighbours.

Conservatories offer gardeners the chance to grow exotic plants, and provide somewhere to relax and admire the garden. Because a conservatory is a connecting room between house and garden, positioning is always limited to the orientation of the house: Garden 7 has a wonderful conservatory on a south-facing wall. To prevent damage to plants and newly laid lawn, building was completed before any of the garden work started. A conservatory heats up

bugs&beasties

All gardens teem with bugs and beasties. Some, for example ladybirds, hoverflies and stag beetles, are good news to gardeners but other are not so welcome.

Slugs and snails can be a problem but, as described in Chapter 5, they provide an opportunity to encourage birds and frogs into the garden.

Greenfly cause damage, but it's nothing compared to what a hungry blue tit can do to these slow-moving aphids.

Vine weevils may be the culprits if you find notches bitten into the edges of leaves, something that often causes consternation among gardeners. They now top the gardeners' wanted list – that's wanted dead and definitely not alive. Seeing vine weevils as a gardening opportunity is initially difficult, but they do force gardeners to look closely at plants and ensure that they're free from vine weevil before buying and importing them into a garden.

Importantly, vine weevils introduce gardeners to biological controls in the garden. Although chemicals are available – one is incorporated in the compost used in containers – the tried and tested use of nematodes is still the best organic way to deal with them. These microscopic worms live naturally in the soil and one particular type, available by mail order or from garden retailers, feeds and reproduces inside vine weevils, killing them in the process. Add these to your soil. Always read the instructions on the packaging carefully and follow them to the letter.

twoinone

One gardener's problem is often another garden's opportunity. The design for Garden 8 incorporated a deep wildlife pond while the neighbours in Garden 7 wanted to raise the level of their flat piece of earth. It made sense to Ali and Chris to remove the adjoining fence temporarily and move the excavated soil from the wildlife garden to the one next door. Cooperation resulted in each of the gardeners sorting out their particular problem while at the same time helping the other one. It is worth consulting your neighbours before embarking on a gardening task. They might be able to help you turn a problem into an opportunity.

quickly so blinds and shading will be necessary. Try to include plenty of ventilation and build as big a structure as your budget or design allows. Once tropical plants start blooming there will never be enough space.

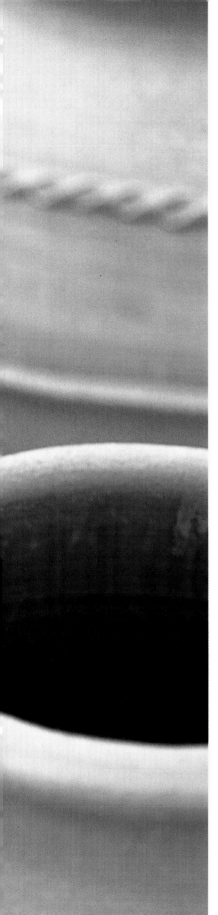

chapter**nine**

pots and ornaments

decoration *n.* an addition that renders something more attractive or ornate.

the gardening neighbours' decorations are sensational. Every garden contains a pleasing work of art, a quiet understated ornament or a subtly placed pot that contributes to the total picture. Decorations can be practical and inspirational or purely aesthetic. For centuries gardeners have been dotting, placing and cramming them into gardens with fantastic results. Victorians adored ornaments and spoils of war provided lasting embellishments in Roman villas, while the gardening neighbours gleaned decorations from battles in garden centres, reclamation yards and on the Internet.

Wherever they originate, ornaments permeate a garden with character. They whisper secrets of the gardener's personality, they emphasize the theme of the garden and they look terrific. But you can't just plonk down a pot, sculpture or bench and expect it to look good. You didn't think it was going to be that easy, did you? Chris and Ali incorporated decorations in the *Gardening Neighbours* gardens from the start of the planning process, and produced stunning effects. The first rule is to be brave and be personal. It is your garden so go for what you want and not what you think others want you to have. The rest is up to your imagination, and your budget.

'Buy old ornaments or just let nature do it for you'
Chris Beardshaw

garden**sculptures**

Sculptures can be made from any material, but natural substances blend and interact with the other elements in a garden. In small plots it is always wise to choose ones that are simple and restrained if total domination of the area is to be avoided. The sculpture commissioned to fit Chris's design for Garden 6, styled to mimic a pebble, is a masterpiece. It wasn't an afterthought, as many ornaments are, but an integral part of the garden from the beginning. It looks impressive but heavy, and indeed would weigh a lot if it was made from solid stone. However, it's hollow and is therefore a manageable weight. A polystyrene core was surrounded by layer upon layer of reconstituted stone, and when the size, texture and colourings were perfect, the polystyrene was burnt out, leaving a pebble shell. This only required the addition of steel rods to support the structure. They are cemented into the soil, preventing any potentially dangerous movement.

As with every other decoration, its placement was important, as the right piece in the wrong setting can ruin a design. A sculpture on a main central axis of a garden, slap bang in front of the eye, will obliterate everything else. Think casual, and place it, almost accidentally, out of the direct eyeline and see the difference. Rising from a gravel stream, the pebble sculpture forms a bold outline softened by clumps of background bamboo. Sunlight plays on

(right) The pebble scuplture in Garden 6 is secured by hidden steel rods and will age with time.

(opposite) A stone from the Lake District adds a personal touch to Garden 2.

its surface creating definite light and dark areas. It is also incredibly tactile and, if not scrubbed clean, will eventually provide a base for beautiful and mysterious lichen growth. This type of sculpture is best placed on its own to act as a focal point. Other decoration would merely detract from its beauty.

In Garden 2 Ali positioned to perfection a sculpture made by the oldest designer in gardening, nature, when she placed a small boulder, aged, shaped and textured by the running waters of the Lake District, in its stream. Water laps gently at its base, occasionally splashing it and creating a multitude of blues, greens, grey and black as the surface changes from wet to dry. It reminds the owner of family ties and memories of childhood.

A sculpture helps a garden to become a place for contemplation, glorious reminiscing and futuristic experimentation.

living**sculpture:**topiary

Trimming and shaping plants is called topiary and produces living sculptures. Usually made from evergreen plants, these add a constant mass to a border, enhancing line, shape and form. They are also easy and great fun to grow.

There are slow and fast ways to create topiary. The slow way involves selecting a suitable specimen and trimming it, sometimes twice a week, to gradually achieve the desired shape, be it peacock, cockerel or watering can. The faster way is to make a wire frame in the shape of the animal or object. Then allow a plant such as one of the ivies (*Hedera* species) to grow through the frame. Trim shoots that grow out of the permitted shape until you have the end result. The fastest way is to buy a ready-shaped specimen from a garden centre or nursery, but these are usually expensive as someone, somewhere, has already done a lot of work.

Garden 3 contains topiary box plants (*Buxus sempervirens*). The conical shapes fit the design perfectly and box is readily adaptable to further training and clipping. It's best to trim plants on cool days, out of the midday sun, to prevent the cut edges of the leaves turning brown.

top**ten**

Grow all the following beauties in multipurpose compost, in pots with drainage holes. The containers can be moved around the garden, to create visual interest in flat spots or where border plants have fizzled out and their replacements haven't come into their own particular blaze of glory. All the plants keep their leaves throughout the year and provide an evergreen backbone to any design.

Box (*Buxus sempervirens*) has small round green leaves that require a trim every month between March and September. Great for small, intricate topiary designs.

Privet (*Ligustrum ovalifolium*) has glossy mid-green leaves that require a trim every week from spring to autumn. Perfect for both small and large topiary designs.

Holly (*Ilex aquifolium*) has shiny, spiky green leaves that require a trim in April, June and August. Best for larger topiary projects.

Bay (*Laurus nobilis*) has large green aromatic leaves that require a trim in May, July and August. A popular choice for lollipop-style trees and larger topiary designs.

Yew (*Taxus baccata*) has compact green leaves that need trimming in April and August. Superb for larger topiary projects.

Lonicera nitida has small green or yellow leaves that require trimming in March, May, July and September. Wonderful for small, fiddly topiary projects.

Ivy (*Hedera* species) has trailing stems of variously coloured and sized leaves that are easily wound around wire frames. Trim whenever shoots protrude out of frame. Marvellous for quick topiary projects of any size.

Elaeagnus pungens 'Maculata' has large green-and-yellow leaves that require trimming in July. Good choice for larger topiary projects.

***Cupressus macrocarpa* 'Goldcrest'** has bright yellow foliage that is easily trimmed in April and August. Superb choice for spirals, cones, spheres and shaped topiary projects.

Osmanthus delavayi has small, glossy dark green leaves that require trimming in April, July and September. Stunning plant, ideal for small topiary projects.

(opposite) Box clipped into a pyramid adds plant value to the design of Garden 3.

plant**containers**

An amazing array of containers is available to suit every garden. They arrive by the ship-load from all over the world, and can add an assortment of moods and feelings to a design. In Garden 4 Ali and the gardening neighbours opted for Cretan jars to import the warmth of the Mediterranean into a north-facing plot. It would be folly to suggest or recommend any one type of pot as everyone has their own views on style, but here are few guidelines to follow when considering containers.

Terracotta: Drainage is fantastic as the pots are porous. However, increased porosity leads to the need for extra watering and the chance that compost may dry out quickly. Pots can also

Different sized pots made from the same material look better than a mish-mash of materials.

containerguidelines

- Ensure that all containers have drainage holes in the base before planting up. The only exception is if you are growing aquatic plants or creating a water feature. If you are, remember that terracotta is porous and will need to be painted with silicon to make it watertight. The same goes for porous stone containers, including concrete.

- Terracotta pots are not naturally frost-proof but ones that have been hand thrown are hardier than machine-made types. A quick way to tell which is which is to look for a straight line or seam running down the outer surface. This is only present if a pot is machine made and is a weak point where frost damage could occur.

- The chances are that pots imported from Crete and other hot countries will not be accustomed to hard frosts, and will need protection over winter to prevent cracking and flaking. Either place them in a frost-free place for winter or cover them with bubble plastic or hessian. The latter doesn't look good in a beautifully designed garden, but will save the pot and any tender roots inside it from irreparable damage.

- Raising a container off the ground will help drainage, and prevent water freezing underneath it which would damage the base. The pebbles and gravel under the Cretan pots in Garden 4 are ideal for this.

- When grouping pots together it's good design policy to stick to the same material, for example all terracotta or all plastic, but vary the sizes. In a small area it looks great to use one large pot rather than a clutter of lots of tiny pots. The clear, distinct lines of a solitary container placed in a border or on the patio can have more impact than a ragtag and bobtail collection of scruffy pots. Don't be afraid to experiment by moving containers around the garden, placing planted and unplanted ones in borders and on patios. Viewing them from different angles will ensure that you get the best from your collection.

discolour, crack and flake in cold weather. Look for frost-proof terracotta and keep receipts just in case.

Wood: If you're buying a hardwood container ensure the wood has come from managed forests. This will help stem the wanton destruction of rainforests by unscrupulous manufacturers. If you're buying softwood, ensure it has been pressure-treated to avoid premature rotting. An inner wrapping of polythene will protect the sides, but don't cover the base as drainage will be impeded.

Glazed earthenware: Many glazed earthenware containers don't have drainage holes and are difficult to drill. Take care, and use eye protection and a sharp drill bit. The pots are great for water features or aquatic plants but are seldom frost-proof. Fantastic colours are available to complement the increasing use of bright paints in garden designs.

Concrete: Pots are heavy, even when empty, but great for leaving to the elements. Mature, weathered, fascinating containers look splendidly

The simplicity of a well-placed watering can adds a personal feel to the garden.

aristocratic in borders and hideaways. The concrete is easily painted to match a mood or change in design. If a container is too heavy to handle, use wheels or a sack truck to move it into its permanent position.

Galvanized steel and other metals: Steel has a clean, modern look, while lead in all its manifestations and intricate container designs takes a garden back to the Victorian age. Copper

Carefully manoeuvre heavy pots into position before filling with compost and plants.

containers – try hunting down jam and marmalade pans in antique shops and at car boot sales – weather to an unmistakable verdigris.

Plastic: Containers are easy to move because they are so lightweight. Tall plants in plastic pots may blow over in windy sites. Plasticotta containers are terracotta lookalikes and are so convincing that people have to touch them to feel the difference. In many cases, manufacturers have even textured the surface to make it look and feel like terracotta. The pots drain well and compost doesn't dry out quite as quickly as it does in their terracotta cousins. There is an infinite choice of colours, sizes and now textures to accompany all garden designs.

statues

The Greeks and Romans loved making statues of their favourite gods, goddesses and members of the current in-crowd. Venus, Neptune, Cupid and innumerable clutches of seraphic cherubs were carved out of stone, marble and clay. And thousands of imprints later, present-day gardeners are using them to great effect.

A well-placed statue at the end of a vista draws the eye and creates a feeling of depth and atmosphere. The view can, however, be a startling one as brand-new marble-look statues are often a dazzling white. Given time, the elements will take the shine off startling statues and give your garden the look and feel of ancient Greece or Rome, but there are other ways to tone down its factory-fresh appearance.

You can encourage the mature look by smearing the surface of statues with a mix of live yoghurt and soil. This rich diet will provide a base for lichens and moss, creating the desired effect in a matter of years rather than decades. Plants can disguise a youthful statue and ivy (*Hedera* species) is used in many designs to tangle and entwine around the base of fake marble figures. A statue placed in a sprawling border looks mysterious surrounded by climbing roses, summer-flowering clematis and honeysuckle. Of course, buying an old statue in the first place will add an air of instant antiquity to your garden.

(above) Wigwam structures give vertical interest to a border, even when bare. When clothed with roses, honeysuckle and clematis they will be outstanding in Garden 8.

(left) Classical, yet factory new, statues and water features will darken in colour and blend beautifully into Garden 8's design.

garden**furniture**

Gardening isn't all weeding, feeding and digging. Sitting back and enjoying your garden is essential, but first you'll have to choose the correct furniture for your weary bones. The choice gets larger every year but as styles and design change, the materials used to make garden furniture stay reassuringly constant.

Aluminium: This is rustproof, lightweight and used in the manufacture of foldaway tables and chairs. When buying aluminium furniture check the springs, nuts and bolts. These are often made from iron or steel and will rust in wet weather. It is therefore better to store tables and chairs away from damp conditions. Gently spraying oil onto the fittings will eliminate rust and seizing-up problems. Cast aluminium is used to make reproduction benches, enabling gardeners to introduce the elegance of a bygone age to their gardens. It has the atmospheric effect and design of cast iron without the drawbacks described below.

Iron: Cast iron furniture was popular in Victorian times but has fallen out of favour because of its weight and the time required to maintain it – it is heavy to lug around a garden and rust appears within a couple of years. Cast iron is inexpensive, tough, but brittle. Wrought iron can be bent into shapes invaluable in benching, and only rusts slowly in the open air. Both types must be painted with anti-rust paint if left in the open air. Because of their weight, large benches and tables tend to stay where they were put in the first place, so try to get it right from the start.

Tubular steel: This is a popular material for hammocks, tables and chairs. The steel itself is inexpensive so the price of the furniture often reflects the quality of the all-important weatherproof coating. This ensures that rust doesn't ruin its appearance and performance. The coating sometimes peels or becomes scratched, exposing the metal. If this happens, treat the exposed steel immediately with an anti-rust agent. Play safe by storing tubular steel furniture indoors in wet weather.

Wood: From a simple log to intricate bench designs, wood is a wonderful material for garden furniture. It can be made from either softwood or hardwood. Softwood is less expensive but can rot quickly without protection, so make sure it has been pressure-treated with preservative. Hardwood is resistant to rot, but always look at labels to ensure it has come from managed forests. Check all wooden furniture for cracks and splinters, and make sure rust-proof screws, nuts and bolts have been used throughout its construction. The furniture is usually flat-packed and is easy to assemble with the correct tools, and a helping hand or two.

It's necessary to treat the surface with wood oils or creams every year to maintain the colour of the wood. If you don't, it will take on an ash-grey appearance as a result of weathering. Wait for furniture to dry out before applying any oils or creams. Treated wood can stay outdoors all winter, but if it isn't being used stand the legs on small blocks to prevent damage by rising damp. Never allow wooden furniture to stand in water.

The integral bench on the circular wooden decking in Garden 4, designed by Ali, includes a simple yet brilliant feature. The top of the

What a seating area – great use of space in Garden 4.

The summerhouse in garden 2 becomes a peaceful retreat to view the garden, once the hard work is done.

seating lifts off to reveal masses of storage space. A great idea for smaller gardens, and one to look for in benches, tables and planters.

Plastic: Injection-moulded plastic produces inexpensive, lightweight and maintenance-free furniture. It is easy to move around a garden and store, but it also blows over in high winds. Colours may fade in bright light, and over a number of years the arms and legs of tables and chairs can become brittle. Treat hard-to-resist offers from manufacturers and retailers with caution. Cheap plastic may only be functional for one year before discoloration renders the surface a dirty grey colour.

Over twenty years ago a mixture of plastics and fillers resulted in resin, a more expensive alternative to plastic but one that is heavier and durable. Furniture comes in a terrific range of styles and colours, with no rust problems. The only maintenance required is a quick wipe with a cloth to remove rain water.

Rattan: This is the choice, along with bamboo and willow, for conservatories and the summer house in Garden 2. Check the quality of the furniture before buying. Strong, solid rattan is a delight whereas the user of thin, flimsy seating never feels safe or comfortable. Rattan is definitely not for permanent outdoor use as damp weather causes moulds and rotting. It looks sensational and inviting in a well-placed summer house overlooking a running stream and magnificently designed garden.

Stone: Stone benches and tables are permanent features because of their weight. Not really designed for lounging and snoozing, they look fantastic as focal points and in strategic positions around a garden. Take care when you move heavier items and make sure they are on a solid base or ground to prevent toppling and sinking. Use a stiff brush to clean stone furniture – but remember that lichen and moss make it look worn and an ever-present part of a garden.

garden**lighting**

Lighting transforms a garden. It extends the leisure time you can spend there, enhances features and plants, and is a good security measure. Little wonder that the *Gardening Neighbours* gardens are superbly lit.

Solar lights are available and are useful when electricity isn't an option. Their output is limited by the amount of sunlight that falls on them, and for strong expression in the garden you will need to consider electricity. Take care when you install it, and if you have any doubts employ a qualified electrician to do the work.

Mains electricity runs through armoured cable via a residual current device (RCD) into weather-proof sockets mounted on secure stakes. The lighting is plugged into the sockets. Don't put these on fence panels or fence posts as they could blow over and sever the cable. The main part of the cable is buried in the soil to prevent accidental damage.

Low-voltage electricity runs from a wall socket into a transformer – both of these are inside the house – then out into the garden. Lights are plugged into the line at special sockets. The cable is housed inside a conduit and buried 45cm (18in) deep in the soil. Place a layer

Wall lights behind specifically designed terracotta covers add a romantic feel to garden 4.

of tiles over the conduit to warn future spade-wielders that the cable is nearby.

There are many lighting options, some requiring mains, some low voltage electricity, and a mixture is preferable to one style as it will create a magical theatre of mystery, shadows, revelations and suspense, regardless of the size of garden.

Floodlights: These illuminate an entire garden rather than an individual feature. Security lights have halogen bulbs and produce strong light that can be harsh, especially if it shines directly into a visitor's eyes. Great for deterring unwanted guests but not ideal at a social gathering.

Spotlights: Use these if you want a beam of light on a particular plant or feature. Two carefully positioned spotlights, both low-voltage, are used to illuminate the statue in Garden 8. Spotlights are also used to highlight the steps in Garden 7 and to light up the troughs in the wavy lawn in Garden 3.

Low-voltage lighting accentuates features in a safe way.

do's&don'ts

✓ **do** have a mixture of lighting types to create a theatre of garden intrigue.

✗ **don't** shine lights directly at eye level.

✓ **do** concentrate on illuminating water features if your budget is limited.

✗ **don't** place lights too close to specimen plants – leaves can burn.

✓ **do** illuminate dangerous steps or beams that are at head height.

✗ **don't** put security lights on the same circuit as garden lighting.

✓ **do** use the flicker from candles to create intimate moods around a dining table in the garden.

✗ **don't** install electricity yourself unless you are a competent electrician.

✓ **do** use low-voltage lights for safety whenever the lighting type allows.

✗ **don't** use coloured lights unless you have experimented with their effect.

✓ **do** have a go with lighting as it will transform your garden.

Up or down, light your pergola uprights to create a feeling of space or magical shadows.

Uplighting: This is created by fixing a light at ground level and shining the beam up into plants or features. Take care to conceal it and protect the bulb from being crushed underfoot.

Downlighting: Use this to focus the eye on chosen objects. Additional background lighting will be essential or it will look as though the object is suspended in the dark. A cleverly positioned downlight can simulate the soft glow of the moon shining through a tree to great effect.

Backlighting: Create this by placing spotlights behind a particular feature. This will produce a black silhouette against a subtly lit background.

Lights in water features: Water responds well to being lit – dancing jewels and gems are created on its surface – and fantastic effects can be achieved with both sophisticated and simple lighting. In Garden 1 the pump in the water has integral lights.

Coloured bulbs: These can make a difference to a lighting scheme, but not always one that's for the best. Plain white light brings out the natural beauty of plants, rocks and other features in the garden, whereas coloured bulbs can cause colour distortions and changes. Experimentation is the best policy.

Torches, flares and candles: These are now as much of an integral part of a garden as plants, decking and pergolas. Candles containing citronella, a natural insect repellent, are great at keeping bugs and beasties away on a warm summer's night, create a romantic atmosphere and are magical behind a sheet of water overflowing the lip of a waterfall. Wall hanging, freestanding and floating candles are all available, easy to use and create an intimate ambience.

general**suppliers**

hand tools
Spear and Jackson
Sheffield
South Yorkshire
0114 281 4242

Stanley Tools
Drakehouse
Sheffield
0114 276 8888

equipment hire
Hewden Hire
For your nearest Hewden Hire
Centre call freephone
0800 371565
www.hewden.co.uk

Jewson
For your nearest branch call
freephone 0800 539766

HSS
For your nearest branch
0845 728 2828
hire@hss.com

Hire It (turf strippers)
01562 744994

wheelbarrows
Haemmerlin
Dudley
West Midlands
01384 243243

lawnmowers
Qualcast
Stowmarket
Suffolk
01449-742000
consumercare.stw@uk.bosch.com

safety shoes
Safety Store
Birmingham
West Midlands
0121 446 4433

gloves
Wilkinson Sword Ltd
London
020 8749 1061

skips
Onyx
0239 266 2210

sprays and hose pipes
Hozelock
Aylesbury
Buckinghamshire
01844 291881

weed killer, compost and fertilizers
The Scotts Company (UK) Ltd
Godalming
Surrey
01483 410210

soil testing
Tenax UK Ltd,
Wrexham Industrial Estate
Wrexham
01978 664667

West Meters
Corwen
Denbighshire
01490 412004

building materials
Ballingers
Leamington Spa
Warwickshire
01926 463000

timber
D.W. Archer Ltd
Banbury
Oxfordshire
01295 272200

wallpaint
Dulux
Slough
Berkshire
01753 691690

fence and decking stain
Cuprinol
01373 475000

pond liner
Midland Butyl (Pond Liner)
Ashbourne
Derbyshire
01335 372133

Brookside Aquatics
Leamington Spa
Warwickshire
01926 612320

pond pumps
Oase (UK) Ltd.
Andover
Hampshire
01264 333225

lighting
Massive UK Ltd
Sittingbourne
Kent
01795 424 442

electrician
Linleigh Electrical
01926 335909

topsoil
Jack Moody
Snareshill
Wolverhampton
01922 417648

J F Tomson
Bishops Tachbrook
Leamington Spa
01926 427349

turf
Teal Turf
Wadborough
Worcester
01905 840279

plants
Manor Farm Nurseries
Charwelton
Northants
01327 260 285

Bernhards
Rugby
Warwickshire
01788 521 177

Notcutts Nurseries
Woodbridge
Suffolk
01394 383 344

Blooms of Bressingham
Bilton Road
Rugby
01788 522 005

Frosts at Millets Farm
Frilford
Oxfordshire
01865 391 923

Highfield Nurseries
01438 812 524

National Herb Centre
01295 690 999

James Coles
0116 241 8394

Pepperidge (wholesalers)
01780 410 720

rendering
Ecotex Coatings
01902 366196

diy stores
Homebase
020 8784 7200

Great Mills
01761 416034

GARDEN 1

Plaslode (Nail Guns)
Fforestfach
Swansea
01792 589800

Baggeridge Brick PLC
Dudley
West Midlands
01902 880555

Celcon Blocks Ltd
Sevenoaks
Kent
01732 880520

BRC Building Products
Stafford
Staffordshire
01785 222288
www.brc-building-products.co.uk

RMC Concrete Products
Redditch
Worcestershire
0870 240 3030

timber
Archer D.W Ltd
Banbury
Oxfordshire
01295 272200

geotextiles
Terram Ltd (Patio Partner)
Pontypool
Gwent
01495 757722
www.terram.co.uk

pond products
Midland Butyl (Pond Liner)
See general suppliers

Brookside Aquatics
See general suppliers

pond pump
Oase (UK) Ltd.
See general suppliers

lighting
Massive UK Ltd
See general suppliers

Linleigh Electrical
See general suppliers

furniture
Fire Island Outdoor Furniture
Redruth
Cornwall
01209 314448

gravel
Bliss Sand & Gravel
Aldridge
West Midlands
01922 743346

Border Hardcore & Rockery Stone Co. Ltd.
Welshpool
Powys
01938 570 375

timber screen
Forest Fencing
Worcester
Worcestershire
01886 812451
Forestfen@aol.com
www.forest-fencing.co.uk

GARDEN 2

Celcon Blocks Ltd
See garden 1

BRC Building Products
See garden 1

RMC Concrete Products
See garden 1

patios and paths
Town and Country Paving Ltd
Littlehampton
West Sussex
01903 776297

geotextiles
Terram Ltd (Patio Partner)
See garden 1

summerhouse
Pounds Garden Buildings
Bewdley
Worcestershire
01299 266000

furniture
Garden Factory
01543 503 709

cobbles and gravel
Bliss Sand & Gravel
See garden 1

**Border Hardcore & Rockery
Stone Co. Ltd.**
See garden 1

york stone bridge
Cox's Architectural Salvage
Moreton-In-Marsh
Gloucestershire
01608 652505
coxs@fsbdial.co.uk
www.salvo.co.uk

GARDEN 3

building materials
Baggeridge Brick PLC
See garden 1

Celcon Blocks Ltd
See garden 1

BRC Building Products
See garden 1

RMC Concrete Products
See arden 1

patios and paths
Blanc de Bierges
Peterborough
Cambs
01733 202566

bbq's
Country Gardens
Thatcham
Berkshire
01635 873700

Weber Stephen Products Ltd
Leyland
Lancs
01772 458580

Black Knight
Maidstone
Kent
01622 671771
sales@blackknightbbq.
demon.co.uk

gravel
Bliss Sand & Gravel
See garden 1

GARDEN 4

geotextiles
TDP Ltd (Plantex)
Wirksworth
Derbyshire

01629 820011
www.tdp.uk.com

lighting
J E Tucker Sculptural Pottery
Solihull
West Midlands
0121 745 7762

decking
Blenheim Palace Decking
0800 917 1166
sales@blenheimpalacedecking.
com

bbq's furniture
Branson Leisure
Harlow
Essex
01279 432151
sales@bransonleisure.co.uk

cobbles and gravel
**Border Hardcore & Rockery
Stone Co. Ltd.**
See garden 1

pots
Rusco
Lechade
Gloucestershire
01367 252754
rusco@lfm.co.uk

Teast Trading
01206 826 453

GARDEN 5

tarmac top mix
Halesowen
West Midlands
0121 550 0043
info@tarmac-central.co.uk

Concrete Pumping (Coleshill)
Coleshill
Birmingham
01675 464291

patios and paths
Marshalls
Southowram
Halifax
0870 120 7474
www.marshalls.co.uk/
drivesandpatios

mosiac tiles
Swedecor Ltd.
Manchester Street
Hull
01482 329 691

GARDEN 6

patios and paths
Woodroyd
Contact James Harte
01226 270025

furniture
Home and Leisure
International
01661 820011

cobbles and gravel
Bliss Sand & Gravel
See garden 1

Border Hardcore & Rockery
Stone Co. Ltd.
See garden 1

sculpture
Marcus Hole
01905 613039

building materials
Baggeridge Brick PLC
See garden 1

Celcon Blocks Ltd
See garden 1

BRC Building Products
See garden 1

RMC Concrete Products
See garden 1

GARDEN 7

arches
Agriframes Ltd
East Grinstead
West Sussex
01342 328644

patios and paths
Town and Country Paving Ltd
See garden 2

geotextiles
Terram Ltd (Patio Partner)
See garden 1

play den
Midland Portable Buildings
Bewdley
Worcestershire
01299 266000

bark
Melcourt Industries
Tetbury
Gloucestershire
01666 502711
www.melcourt.co.uk
mail@melcourt.co.uk

GARDEN 8

patios and paths
Tarmac TopPave Ltd
Wergs Hall Road
Wolverhampton
08702 413450

hurdles
Hawkins Salmon
Brackley
Northants
01280 701880

furniture
Encompass
Compton
West Sussex
02392 631859
encomfaa@fsbdial.co.uk
www.encompassco.com

pergola
Forest Fencing
See garden 1

water feature pot
Teast Trading
See garden 4

turf
Rolawn Medallion cultivated
turf supplied by
Rolawn (Turf Growers) Ltd
Elvington
York
01904 608661
info@rolawn.co.uk
www.rolawn.co.uk

index

Numbers in italic refer to illustrations